TRANSCENDING ALL UNDERSTANDING:
THE MEANING OF
CHRISTIAN FAITH TODAY

WALTER KASPER

Transcending All Understanding:

The Meaning of Christian Faith Today

Translated by Boniface Ramsey, O.P.

COMMUNIO BOOKS

IGNATIUS PRESS   SAN FRANCISCO

Title of the German original:
Was alles Erkennen übersteigt:
Besinnung auf den christlichen Glauben
© 1987 Verlag Herder
Freiburg im Breisgau

Cover by Roxanne Mei Lum

With ecclesiastical approval
© 1989 Ignatius Press, San Francisco
ISBN 0–89870–256–9
Library of Congress catalogue number 89–83497
Printed in the United States of America

To my father
on his eighty-sixth birthday

CONTENTS

FOREWORD

The following reflections come from different lectures given on various occasions. They were revised and reworked for publication. It goes without saying that they do not claim to be a complete presentation of what is customarily dealt with in a theological treatise on faith. They address a few obstacles to the clarification and deepening of personal faith in today's world. I am sincerely grateful to all those who by their questions, objections, suggestions and, not least, personal faith witness have contributed to producing these reflections.

Tübingen, on the Feast of the Epiphany of the Lord, 1987

Walter Kasper

TRANSLATOR'S NOTE

The German word *Glaube*, which appears through-
out this work, can be translated as either faith or
belief. It has been translated in these pages as the
context seems to suggest, but where either English
word appears it is a rendering of the one German
term.

This translation was done at the urging of
Sister Miriam of the Cross, O.P., prioress of
the Dominican Monastery of Mary the Queen in
Elmira, New York. The translator wishes to
thank her for her encouragement, and he offers
his efforts to her as a token of friendship.

B.R.

I

Faith Challenged

A Burning Issue

"The handing on of the faith" is a problem almost everywhere today and has become a deep crisis. This is the burning issue for the contemporary Church. Despite the greatest efforts and the best will, faith is ever more in danger of evaporating in our modern and postmodern world. Less and less does it appear to be a determinative influence on life and reality. Its power to witness and its ability to be passed on seem to be growing weaker.

Not only numerous pastors and religion teachers but parents as well are asking: What is going to happen? How can we confront this crisis? Can we confront it at all? Every alert observer of Western society in particular can see a massive decline in religious practice and the disappearance of religious signs and symbols in the public forum. Believers find themselves nearly everywhere in a diaspora situation, standing guard at a forgotten post, so to speak.

Faith Itself Is Questioned

One thing seems certain: the crisis runs so deep and is so all-encompassing that it is not enough merely to call upon more effective and appealing methods and improved structures in order to hand on the faith. A discussion about external reforms is undoubtedly necessary, but it may not be conducted in a superficial way, for that would itself be a sign of diminished faith. It is not simply the handing on of the faith but faith itself that is in question today, not simply the "how" of its being taught but the "what" and "why" of faith. Faith itself is being challenged.

In this respect it is not only a matter of others' faith or of the next generation's faith. It is a matter of *our* faith! If it were more convincing, more infectious, more burning, then we would probably not have to be worried about its being handed on. What we need in particular, therefore, are living witnesses of faith. Only faith as it is lived is convincing.

Theologians have little to do with this. In such a situation theology can only offer modest assistance. A lived and living faith cannot be demonstrated to anyone; it must be witnessed to. In this respect a person can certainly argue carefully on behalf of faith and defend it against its intellectual adversaries. This is the way that the Christian is supposed to give an account of the hope that is in us (see 1 Pet 3:15). In addition, the theologian can attempt to reflect on "the length and breadth, the height and depth" of the mystery of Christ, who lives in our hearts through faith, and to expound the whole inner wealth of the faith. But while doing this he will see time and again that the love of Christ transcends all understanding (see Eph 3:17–19).

In what follows we want to pose the question in this decisive way: What does faith mean? What is faith about? What is our faith founded on? What do we believe in, as far as our faith is concerned? We are asking thus about the essence, act, content and basis of Christian belief. Finally, we are also asking about the community of believers, the Church.

But What Does Faith Mean?

To put the question in this way is absolutely necessary. The word *believe* is very rich in possible meanings, even in everyday speech. If we say, for instance: "I believe that it will rain tomorrow", what we mean is: I have some reasons, to be sure, but I am not certain. Belief here means a mere opinion and conjecture. Otherwise it can stand for credulity; blind faith; unenlightened, intellectually comfortable, authority-oriented behavior and even false belief and superstition. But the word *believe* can also express confidence, trust and fidelity. If I say, for instance: "I believe you", then belief is linked not to some merely conjectured fact but to a person upon whom I bestow trust because I am certain of his trustworthiness. In this case belief does not express an unsure knowledge but rather a deep certainty founded on personal trust.

Belief is consequently a word with many possible meanings. Given these many meanings, the word *believe* can be misused. The legitimate and aberrant forms of belief—namely, faith and superstition—are often close to one another and are frequently confused with one another. One can take advantage of the willingness to believe and the power of faith in young people in particular, thus abusing their trust. Totalitarian systems show that they are especially adept and subtle in this regard, and the new youth cults demonstrate the urgency of this danger even in our own society.

Not only is everyday speech multileveled in its use of *believe*, but so is religious and Christian speech. If a Christian confesses: "I believe", he does not simply intend to say by this that God exists. Even the demons believe this, as the Letter of James says, and they tremble (see James 2:19).

By saying such a thing a Christian is by no means expressing a lack of certain knowledge. On the contrary, he is declaring the highest personal certainty. His belief is a matter of fixity and content, touching on the foundation and goal of his existence. This trust, however, is based on the completely determined content of faith—on faith in God's history with mankind, on the Incarnation of God, on the cross and Resurrection of Jesus Christ and on the efficacious presence of God's Holy Spirit in the word and sacrament of the Church. In faith, consequently, the act of faith and the content of faith must be distinguished. Augustine, in fact, differentiated three meanings of religious faith—the content-oriented *belief that* (*credere Deum*, to believe that God exists), the *belief of trust* (*credere Deo*, to believe God in the sense of trusting God) and the *belief of the journey* (*credere in Deum*, to journey toward God, and to do this in common with all the members of the Body of Christ).

But the theological understanding of faith has often been narrowed down to the first aspect. Faith was often one-sidedly understood as *belief that* and as the affirmation of propositions and of supernatural realities. If belief is understood only in this narrow content-oriented fashion, then the crisis of faith consists in the fact that nowadays even many baptized Christians no longer accept all the Church's teachings with respect to many

critical points of doctrine—for example, the existence of angels and demons, the Virgin Birth and
sexual morality. The knowledge of the faith has in
many ways fallen to a new low today. This is a
very serious phenomenon, for a faith without a
content is an untenable faith, without an object in
the twofold sense of the word. It quickly evaporates
and is in danger of getting confused beyond recog-
nition with other positions, movements, ideologies
and utopias. But if the content-oriented aspect is
absolutized, then the handing on of the faith and
the teaching of the faith give the impression of
being indoctrination. It is not only the enlightened
modern person with his concern for freedom who
resists this; the truly believing person also resists
it. He knows that belief is much more than the
affirmation of propositions such as one finds in a
catechism. Belief is also an act and a carrying out;
indeed, it is an attitude that determines one's whole
life. An aspect of the contemporary crisis of faith
that should not be underestimated is the fact that
many of the fundamental attitudes of belief—
reverence, humility, trust and devotion—have
become foreign to us. The act of faith and the
content of faith have both come under attack
today.

The Blurring of Outlines

There were, to be sure, always dangers, temptations and even persecutions for believers. But today the problem posed for the faith has taken on a new characteristic. The situation is dramatic not least of all because belief and unbelief no longer stand in contrast with one another as clearly identifiable entities. The clear outlines are blurred because belief itself is often pulled apart and attacked and threatened in its substance from within, while unbelief, at least in our Western society, for the most part no longer comes across today as militant. The self-assuredness of belief has been destroyed along with that of unbelief; it too has become sceptical and, in the end, indifferent.

In this increasingly all-embracing but also vague and anonymous atmosphere of indifference the points of contact between belief and unbelief often seem imperceptible and go almost unnoticed. Rarely has the unbeliever succeeded in disguising himself as well as he can in today's Babylonian confusion of languages. Nothing is clearly asserted anymore, nothing is directly denied anymore but everything is instead redefined, restated and re-interpreted. The result is that the differences between belief and unbelief are dissolving. This can go so far that all of a sudden atheism is discovered in Christianity, and the thesis is proposed that "only an atheist can be a good Christian and only a Christian can be a good atheist" (E. Bloch). Thus unbelief suddenly appears devout because it is open, tolerant and engaged. It has itself become a new kind of religion with an uncanny power of attraction. Strong confessional faith is then often laid aside as narrow.

It goes without saying that the word of faith should not be spoken in a falsely self-assured and intolerant fashion. Such an attitude usually arises not from strong but from weak faith. It should rather be said that the faithful must ask themselves today in a new and deeper way: What does faith really mean? What is faith about? What is the binding content of faith? How does faith justify and substantiate itself? Why believe and confess one's faith at all? How can one hand on the faith in a living way? How can we make understandable again—first to ourselves and then to others—the fact that believing is beautiful, that faith is a great gift to be passed on and that it is the salvation of mankind?

II

Faith Called into Question

Most broadly understood, faith is an essential element in all religions. Religious men of every era have taken for granted that the reality that we can lay hold of with our senses is by no means the deepest and certainly not the only reality. They are convinced that sensibly experienced reality exists only insofar as it participates in an entirely other and more encompassing reality that is called the reality of the holy. For them the holy is a *mysterium tremendum et fascinosum*—that is, a mystery that simultaneously arouses fear and fascination. Consequently, religion always includes a trusting in and a building upon realities that are of an extra-sensory kind. They are the religious man's point of reference and his consolation in his life's anguish and need. But not infrequently the holy and divine is an object of fear and of fright. It is a deeply ambivalent phenomenon.

Faith's Loss of Function

Our average present-day conviction is radically distinct from this human conviction concerning religion. For our present-day consciousness, the material and economic reality that is ascertainable by the senses is the true reality. Everything else is derived from it, and everything else is measured by it. Indeed, all of spiritual and religious reality is often seen merely as a reflection of, a projection of or a surrogate for experiences and needs accessible to the senses or societal concerns. Or at best it is given second place alongside so-called concrete problems.

To be sure, there have been objections to religious tradition ever since the time of the ancient Sophists and the philosophical Sceptics. Nonetheless, the present-day widespread secularistic view of reality that has been alluded to is, from the standpoint of human and cultural history, a recent phenomenon. As a conviction of the mass of the people it is hardly a hundred years old.

Christianity and theology are not guiltless with respect to this development. In teaching and still more in private and social life, as the Second Vatican Council itself acknowledges, the true face of God was often more veiled than witnessed to as living. In the late Middle Ages and at the beginning of the modern period the act of faith, which was originally and which is ultimately a simple affair, evolved into numerous individual content-oriented questions that were often completely irrelevant for practical life. Faith gradually turned into a structure that, because of its many accretions, was extremely complicated, hardly transparent any longer to the ordinary Christian and no longer a place in which he found himself at home. In addition, in the Middle Ages faith in God often became faith in an arbitrary God who could even deceive and lead men astray but whom they were nonetheless obliged to obey blindly. A faith such as this could no longer be experienced as a liberating reality; it was seen as a thing cloaked in authoritarianism, oppressing man's freedom and dignity. Against this one-sidedly objectivizing and authoritarian understanding of faith men had to protest for the sake of their human dignity.

The protest came first of all from the Reformers. Luther reproached the faith of mere affirmation; for him faith was trust (*fiducia*) in God's grace alone for the sake of Christ. Against Erasmus, however, whom he considered a sceptic, Luther also clearly stated that faith was expressed with the utmost certainty in firm propositions (*assertiones*). Hence it came about that from the roots of the Reformation there later sprang up a new scholastic system. Pietism confronted it with the demand for a simple and uncomplicated faith of the heart. With this a chord was struck that echoed later in romanticism and that has returned today in numerous tendencies—faith as a presentiment of and a feeling for the unconditional, faith as a

personal experience (often remaining quite vague)
of divine mystery. Pietism thus unintentionally
prepared the way for the Enlightenment and for
its critique of a positive, concrete, historical revelation with a concrete, specifically Christian
content-oriented faith. What was left over after
the Enlightenment was a general human faith in a
highest Being that, because of its lack of content,
would soon have to dissolve in thin air. A philosopher like Hegel could not refrain from pouring
over this all his biting scorn.

But there remains the question as to how and
why this uncompelling religion of the Enlightenment could have gotten as far as it did. There are
numerous reasons. One of them certainly lies in the
advance of the natural sciences, as they were understood in the eighteenth and nineteenth centuries—
namely, as related to a mechanistic view of the
world. They succeeded better and better in ex-
plaining the phenomena of reality apart from God.
The "hypothesis of a God" had become superfluous. But Christians themselves were in good
measure guilty for the changed situation. In the
religious wars of the sixteenth century that followed
upon the Reformation, the society of the time fell
to pieces. The Christian religion had lost its func-
tion as the glue that held everything together. It
even became the occasion for conflict and war,
which led society to the brink of ruin. The only

thing that was left over when, for the sake of peace and survival, religion was declared a private matter and the public order had been placed on a basis common to all and binding on all, irrespective of the different confessional emphases of Christian belief, was human reason, common to all.

Thus it is that for many reasons a culture arose that sought to explain the world and life purely autonomously and solely from their immanent and this-worldly causes. Faith in God seemed to many to have become superfluous. It was often placed more or less in the realm of the purely personal, private and even intimate. In the public consciousness it more and more lost its foothold and its plausibility. It became a mere fragment, a segment alongside other realms that were now appearing in the foreground, and finally it was marginalized. Thus personal faith was less and less supported and encouraged by public opinion. It was put off by itself and quite frequently had to accommodate itself to the completely different mental framework of the time.

The Faith Critically Interrogated and Superseded

The Enlightenment wanted to protect the dignity of man and order and peace among men by making human reason the point of departure, the criterion and the forum to which everything, even faith, would be responsible. Everything was supposed to be grasped reasonably and be reasonably formulated; no authority was supposed to be accepted untried. Faith itself was placed under the rule of reason and of a completely determined empirical ideal, under the ideal of the "clear and distinct idea"—namely, under the ideal of what we recognize as clear and distinct and what we could prove in a mathematical and geometrical way. If this is the measure that is used, then faith may be suspected (according to Kant) of being a deficient and degenerate form of knowledge, a second-class knowledge. In the most benign interpretation faith could, as with Lessing or Hegel, qualify as a still incomplete anticipation of knowledge, which would be superseded.

Finally, Auguste Comte, the father of modern positivism and the representative of an almost limitless optimism of progress, formulated the famous "law of three stages": the age of religion is brought to a close by that of metaphysics, which in its purely abstract and philosophical fashion questions its most basic principles, and this age of metaphysics is then superseded by that of modern science. This last, according to Comte, in contrast to the two preceding epochs, has knowledge about the true cause of things. Thus the scientific epoch could solve more problems in a short period and do more for the good of humanity than could be accomplished in all the previous centuries. Faith is now enlightened, superseded and abolished.

Dialectical materialism, which is the official party and state ideology in the Marxist-socialist-oriented countries of eastern Europe, has taken over many elements of this enlightened, positivistic critique of religion and revelation. According to it, religious faith is the result of the experience of human alienation. In this situation men create an opium for themselves in religion. Religion reposes on a fantastic and absurd reflection of an absurd reality and leads to an unprovable conviction concerning the existence of supernatural, immaterial beings and forces. It is nonetheless actually only making an absolute and a fetish of incomprehensible albeit elementary forces at work in social process. According to this ideology, religious faith stands in unbridgeable opposition to knowledge and science, which repose on an objective and scientific analysis of man and his relationship to nature and to society.

Even in modern Western neopositivism and in critical rationalism the arguments of the Enlightenment may be found in modified form. In the view of H. Albert, every search for an unconditional and ultimate proof leads to a trilemma. That is to say, one of three possibilities faces a person: either, in the course of his search for ultimate proofs, he keeps going back in an infinite regression; or, in a logical circle, he presupposes what must be proven in the proof; or he breaks off the process more or less arbitrarily and appeals to ultimate and self-evident principles that therefore have no further need of proof, which is the procedure of dogmatism. Albert sets critical rationalism in opposition to this. It does not behave as self-assuredly as the old rationalism did. It is essentially more modest and only wants to make provisional statements from time to time, which are at the basis of a broader critique. Here truth is a goal that is striven after and that is being approached ever more closely over the course of history but that is never ultimately attained. This amounts, however, to a fundamental scepticism with regard to every ultimate truth and proof.

Thus religious faith that reposes on an ultimate certitude appears to many as a leftover from earlier ages and as a fossil from another and long-past era. For them it belongs to the childhood of the human race and is unworthy of men who have become adult, mature and critical. Man come of age must solve his own problems and thereby, as Freud taught, make do without any ultimate consolation.

But this sceptical modesty concerning the self did not stop there. The modern critique of religion, in its rationalistic urge to clarify, also sought to solve the riddle of how such a thing as religion could have come about in the first place. It wanted thus to lay bare the mechanisms of religious convictions. That so universal a phenomenon as religion reposed only on the trickery of priests, as many Enlightenment figures thought, was in the long run not very convincing. Consequently an attempt was made to understand faith in God as a projection of the divine dignity and greatness proper to mankind itself (Feuerbach). It was held to be the satisfaction, by wish and compensation, of unrealizable needs and longings (Freud); a misguided protest and a sanction against inequitable relationships, the opium of the people (Marx); an expression of resentment against a too-short life (Nietzsche). Marx condensed this critique of religion neatly: it is not religion that makes man but man who makes religion. Contemporary atheism wants to be humanism.

The Obscurity of God

It has been said that the "revolt against the Church" of the sixteenth century led in the eighteenth century to a "revolt against Christ and Christianity" and in the nineteenth and twentieth centuries to a "revolt against God". This explanation of what happened is certainly too simple. The complex of causes of modern atheism and indifferentism is much too complicated for it to be reducible to a single factor.

The contemporary process of autonomization and secularization can also not be characterized simply as a falling away from God. Christianity also had a part to play in this. There was the Bible itself, which enjoined man to distinguish between God and the world and not to confuse God with the world and with the world's forces, thereby turning them into idols. Thus even in the Old Testament the way was being prepared for a worldly and rational view of reality. The mainstream Christian tradition was basically as little inimical to reason and enlightenment as was the Bible. Quite the contrary! Thus we as Christians do not need, even today, to see ourselves as fundamentally antimodern, "medieval" and reactionary. We may and should understand the good that the contemporary world has brought with it—particularly the general awareness of freedom, of human dignity and of human rights —as a secular piece of the Christian heritage, which we must defend today along with all men of goodwill. The last Council spoke expressly of a legitimate autonomy in the realm of secular affairs, and it solemnly affirmed and endorsed freedom of religion, which is the most basic of all human rights.

A perversion occurs only when human freedom is seen not simply as unconditional but even as absolute and when its constitutive finality goes unrecognized. When it is no longer recognized that man is, in the freedom of his conscience, oriented to a divine plan that has been given him, then the result is a megalomania that expresses itself in a frenzied will to make and to dominate, which today imperils the life and survival of mankind.

It was thus not his taking seriously of human freedom, but rather the usurped and sinister freedom of a "superman", that led Nietzsche to the famous conclusion that God was dead. For Nietzsche, God had to be dead so that the "superman" could live. But is the "superman" really a man? In our century the proclamation of the death of God led consistently to the proclamation of the death of man and to the attempt to do away with the ancient European human rights. The freedom that atheism promised never in fact came.

In the meantime a deathly void has taken God's place; noisy activity is distracting, but it can never fill the emptiness. This activity, however, completely dulls the heart and renders it insensitive to the traces and signs of God, to God's voice in the voice of the conscience.

In this sense Nietzsche's words about the death of God seem to many to imply a just assessment with respect to our Western civilization. What they ordinarily take Nietzsche's words to mean is not that God does not exist but rather that his existence no longer carries any weight at all. Men carve out their own fortunes for themselves and push aside the rest, the enduring questions, in the anxiety and activity of day-to-day living. Indifferentism of this sort is much more dangerous than that militant atheism for which God continues to be a problem and something to fight against. For indifferentism, however, God is dead in the sense that life no longer radiates from him, that he no longer provokes and inspires. The numerous small questions, sometimes oppressing and sometimes fascinating, become so overpowering that there is no more room for the larger questions. Thus God is dead more because of the silence in his regard than because he is being talked about. It was in this sense that Buber spoke of the obscurity of God.

This obscuring of the spiritual horizon, this religious eclipse, does not go unnoticed by believers. They cannot simply withdraw from the prevailing atmosphere. The doubt of unbelief gnaws at their own hearts often enough. But if their faith were more stimulating and provocative, it would really change their lives and the world, and it would certainly provide others with something to think about. But often there is nothing else for us to say except: "Lord, I believe; help my unbelief" (Mk 9:23). And so, living close to today's questions and needs, we have to explore new approaches and ways to faith for ourselves and for others.

III

Ways to Faith

There are many different ways to faith. Each person has his own faith history. Basically, there are as many approaches to faith as there are believers. A particular experience, an encounter, a word, a book—any of these can be the point of departure for a decisive turn to faith. There is also, of course, the way of thought and reflection, which we want to pursue in the following pages. As thoughtful and mature men, we are supposed to give an account of our faith even in intellectual fashion to ourselves and to others. In this respect we must first leave open how deeply this way of thought leads into the realm of faith. We must never set up stop signs beforehand when it comes to thought, and even less must we place restrictions on thought.

A Situation That Stimulates Reflection

The self-assured positivistic and rationalistic belief in progress that was common in previous centuries and decades is already outmoded in our day. It has collapsed or is on the point of collapsing. It is not a question, to be sure, of whether considerable progress has been made or not. One need only think, for example, of the progress in medicine that no reasonable person today would wish to renounce. In addition, there is in the modern democracies a progress in the awareness and the realization of human freedom, which is worth defending with all one's strength. For a Christian faith that understands itself properly, an enmity toward science and progress is no way out of the present crisis; that is something that we should leave to the modern sects. On the contrary, we hope for still more developments that will bring blessings with them. Our program cannot be a restoration of previous conditions. Rather, now that we have come up against the critique of Christian belief, it is a matter of learning from the many mistakes of the past and so coming to a purer and deeper understanding of the faith. For this the possibilities are good.

It is not progress, indeed, but rather faith in progress that belongs in the dustbin of history. This fell apart in the inferno of the two world wars. It became utterly unworthy of belief in the face of the atomic peril that resulted from progress, negative ecological developments, increasingly limited resources and much more. Men today know again about the dialectic of enlightenment and progress—that is, about the regression that is inherent to progress. For everything, even progress, has its price. Technological progress, when it is isolated and absolutized, leads to a one-dimensional thought and life in which the reason of the heart and the culture of love wither away. An absolutized rationality itself becomes irrational in the end, and mere functionality must necessarily turn inhuman. Thus even science and technology can sink into repressive ideologies. Is not the triumph of the modern accompanied by and even partly made possible by the suffering of many on account of exploitation and oppression?

The dissatisfaction with the progress of technological civilization first became apparent in the so-called student revolt at the end of the sixties and the beginning of the seventies. This was fundamentally a kind of cultural revolution with far-reaching effects on the social consciousness that are still being felt today. This new thrust of enlightenment and emancipation was directed not least of all against the remains of religious tradition that had survived up until then but that were being defamed as taboos. The internal utopias that briefly took their place, however, swiftly disappeared. In the end their senselessness and their fecklessness were completely evident.

The reaction was and is a new religious wave— Eastern meditation practices, healing movements, youth cults, psychological techniques, fundamentalistic tendencies (especially in Islam), occultism and spiritualism, astrology, belief in reincarnation and New Age thought, all tied up with both apocalyptic anxiety and a hope in a far-reaching transformation of the contemporary situation. This and much else show that the talk, which was current twenty years ago, of continual and progressive secularization through science and technology has in the meantime become outdated as a result of subsequent events. American sociologists have long since replaced the thesis of continual and progressive secularization with that of the persistence of religion.

But we must be careful. The present religious awakening is a highly diffuse and ambivalent phenomenon that does not necessarily make things easier for the churches and for their teaching of the faith. It can even be a dangerous competitor and adversary, and this is evident in the worldwide and rapid growth of sects and not least of all in the so-called youth cults. The turnaround in the general atmosphere has, to be sure, produced a stronger demand for spirituality, but the new irrationalism—and even antirationalism—is very critical and threatening.

The present situation poses a serious question to Christians and to the churches. They have to ask themselves whether they are guilty of having

created a vacuum that could be filled by such
ideologies, utopias, religious sects and esoteric
religions.

In any event, Christian faith is being questioned
anew today—and not merely in its sociological
and political relevance, which is not uppermost in
people's minds, but in its religious substance. God
and the difference between true and false religious-
ness are now the themes. It goes without saying
that social responsibility and action-oriented love
belong to true religion and to true faith. But
Christian faith must also give its answer in a
rational way to the new situation, while ob-
jectively taking into consideration the questions
and objections. That alone is consonant with the
Christian tradition and with human dignity.

The Reasonableness of Faith

The objection that Christianity is not to be taken
seriously because it is "only" based on faith and
not on personal experience and incontrovertible
proof is not new to us today. The pagan philosopher
Celsus had already argued in this fashion in the
second half of the second century. Origen, the
most famous theologian of the third century and
perhaps the greatest theologian of all time, said
that, on the contrary, no one could do anything

without faith. With this Origen took up an important insight of the philosophy of the day, which had already been established by Aristotle and was represented especially in the contemporary popular philosophy of Stoicism. These philosophers had said that in his perceptions and in his behavior every man speaks out of presuppositions, basic principles and fundamental options. He cannot always derive these from higher principles. These basic principles must rather be assumed in a kind of faith and be shown reasonable in the concrete experience and activity of life. They must be verified, but they cannot be proven.

Augustine, the greatest Church Father of the West, argued similarly 150 years later. Against the same objection he too showed that every man and each thought assume presuppositions. I cannot even prove that my parents are really my parents; yet it does not occur to me to doubt this, and the refusal to give my parents their due respect would be seriously immoral behavior.

Even rationalism makes such presuppositions. For precisely the man who wants to understand and establish everything in a rational way must, in the face of so much in the world that is irrational, first believe somehow in the sense of rationality. Whoever gives value only to the sensibly material and to what is positively ascertainable, however, assumes, whether he wants to or not, a point of view that he can never establish from sensible experience and in a positivistic way. For the fact that only the positively ascertainable is real can never be positivistically proven. This bears even on the radical sceptic. For whoever says that a person must and can doubt everything and that there is no certitude regarding the truth is himself making a statement that implies certitude. This is quite apart from the fact that there are even statements that sceptics do not doubt and that, in common sense, they cannot doubt. These touch not only on mathematical truths but also on one's own existence and one's own thinking. "I think and therefore I am" was consequently for Augustine and later, in a much more radical way, for Descartes the keystone of all certitude. But whoever with certitude excludes ultimate certitude contradicts himself and immunizes himself very uncritically against all criticism.

Thus the Church Fathers and the medieval Scholastics were justifiably convinced that faith precedes reason; therefore it is not rationally derived. But faith is not on that account irrational; it is in fact extremely rational. For it seeks and demands understanding, and, indeed, it makes possible human understanding (*fides quaerens intellectum*).

Reality as an Absolute

The thesis of a presupposed faith is even more deeply founded today. The self-assured point of departure of the modern era with respect to human reason and freedom has been more and more questioned in postidealism since the second third of the last century. It was already clearly stated in "the" modern philosopher, Kant, what then in the late philosophy of Schelling, of Kierkegaard and Nietzsche and in our own century with Jaspers and Heidegger became generally accepted—namely, that the reason and freedom from which modern man derives everything and to which he relates everything are themselves not derivative. Man is an ultimate being; he is himself presupposed as underived. Indeed, reality as a whole is for us underived and absolute. Consequently it is not a matter of asking simply: What is? but first of all: Why is there anything at all rather than nothing?

The insight into the underived facticity of reality has created a fundamentally new situation for thought. It does not lead directly to faith in God. It can as well lead to completely other options, such as a feeling of absurdity or a sense of fatalism. In any event, however, it leads to a new personal modesty with respect to thought, for it makes universal systems impossible from the very start.

Thus it is more clearly recognized today than it was before that there is no presuppositionless thought, and that rather each point of departure for thinking and understanding is linked to a particular historical preunderstanding, to options and also to interests. This does not mean that now everything is possible in the sense of the postmodern "anything goes". The distinction between yes and no, true and false, good and evil cannot be given up unless men want to give up being human. Hence it is a matter of justifying one's presuppositions and of confronting them with reality time and again. Everything else leads either to an ideological turning in upon oneself or to a pure nihilism that no longer permits any reasonable communication.

The faith that accepts and affirms reality as absolute and presupposed and as coming from God and that does so in creaturely humility and gratitude can argue in twofold fashion in this new situation: it can start from the underived nature of the individual, and it can refer to the incomprehensibility of the whole of reality. Let us ask, then, where and how far these arguments lead.

Faith Means Accepting Something on Another's Testimony

The individual is ultimately impenetrable to reason. No grain of sand in the desert is completely like any other; each is unique. In no individual case can we determine every concrete particularity. Every man is not only quantitatively but also qualitatively unique. The existence of each individual human being is untransferable and incommunicable. Man is neither a mere bundle of physical, psychical, social and other functions nor a particular instance of the universal. Each one is a unique I, a unique person. That is the basis of his inalienable dignity. Man is an end unto himself. Thus no man fits into an abstract scheme any more than he fits into positivistic determinations, however correct they may be.

Consequently, in our relations with other men we are always dependent on trust and faith. We have to accept many things, most things, on others' testimony without the possibility of looking at the matter for ourselves. The only thing that we can and must do is scrutinize the trustworthiness of the witnesses. Augustine points out to us, as we have seen, that we could never love and trust our parents if we did not believe that they were our parents. We have good grounds for accepting that they really are such, but it can never be proved with certainty. We believe them and others. If we ask in this case and in others whether other persons are trustworthy, then we have to trust them until there is evidence to the contrary. Reasonable human interaction would otherwise be impossible. Faith and trust are hence the basis for human interaction.

From what has been said there emerges a first definition of faith (although it is still rather general because it is common to mankind): faith means accepting something on another's testimony and holding it for true.

Faith of this sort is the presupposition for all scientific progress. If we want to further our knowledge, we cannot always start anew. We must instead lay hold of the treasure of experience and knowledge of those who came before us. We must let ourselves be directed by a teacher whom we trust and whom we believe to be knowledgeable, so as to be able ourselves to know, to understand, to think further and to investigate further. Whoever wishes to learn must have faith, as Aristotle observed. History and law in particular depend on witnesses and testimony and cannot get along without faith of this sort. It goes without saying that we depend on faith with regard to questions that are existentially more important in a way that we do not with regard to problems that admit of scientific certitude, however important they may also be. Human interaction, human trust, human fidelity and love depend on such faith.

Transcendental Faith

In addition to the impenetrability of the individual there is an impenetrability to reason on the part of the whole of reality. As unique as man is, he is nonetheless at the same time open to other men and ultimately to the whole of reality. He is, as the anthropologists say, "open to the world". In contrast to the brute animal, he is not limited to a particular environment to which he reacts with sure instincts. The environment of man is reality as a whole. He is of his very nature, in the first place, without home or orientation in the world. He must create his environment for himself and give himself orientation. Therefore he inquires after the "whereto" and the "wherefrom" of life and reality, after the reason and the meaning of being; he inquires after every aspect of reality. This questioning can certainly be forgotten and pushed aside for long periods, but situations are continually arising when we find ourselves asking: Where is everything actually going?

This sense of the whole cannot be grasped in definitions; if it could, then it would itself have to be situated on a still wider horizon of meaning. The whole is thus like the horizon, which embraces everything, into which a person walks while it goes with him but which is never reached. From the purely human point of view, therefore, there is essentially no final answer to the question of the meaning of man. Whenever we have reached our goal, we are also faced with "the melancholy of fulfillment" (E. Bloch) and with the realization that this goal was not the ultimate fulfillment and complete happiness. A man cannot catch up with himself and with his longing for happiness. Here we stand before a final dilemma and a final mystery of our being. However the response to the question of the meaning of the whole may turn out, it must be dared and in the broadest sense of the word be believed. But nowadays we often hear of mistrust as a fundamental presupposition of life.

With this we stand once more before the insight of ancient and patristic philosophy. The ultimate presuppositions of our thought and of our life are not at all demonstrable; they must be accepted with a kind of faith, and then they can be proven in day-to-day living and in the phenomenon of reality. Faith—in this as yet not specifically Christian but rather general sense—is not a deficient mode of knowledge, no mere opinion or surmise, no un-enlightened, naive and uncritical, gullible acceptance. It is, instead, the fundamental act and the fundamental accomplishment of human existence. Speaking philosophically, B. Welte refers to this as transcendental faith. By this is meant that faith is the presupposition of and the condition for categoric knowledge (that is, knowledge of the individual) and that it makes this possible, without ever being absorbed in any of these acts.

Faith thus understood is something completely different from a closed-off ideological position. It is rather the most radical openness and breadth. It is the taking on of life in its openness to the future. It is that courage to be, to use Tillich's expression, without which we could never live in human fashion. It is faith in life and in the meaning of life. It is, above all, faith in freedom. For neither one's own freedom nor anyone else's can be proven. Freedom is a permanent article of faith for mankind (Schelling). Woe to us if this faith is ever extinguished. Humanity would then be ultimately lost.

Antechambers of Faith

Both the individual and the whole are, in the last resort, impenetrable to our reason. Pascal, who was a mathematician of genius, gave a striking description of the situation of man, set in the middle between two extremes:

> This is our real situation. This is what makes us incapable of certain knowledge and uncomfortable without knowledge. Occupying a vast middle posi-

tion, we are driven, always in suspension and pushed from one extreme to another. Whenever we wish to attach ourselves to and stay at a particular boundary post, it wavers and disappears, and if we pursue it, it slips from our grasp, escapes us and flies off in an endless flight. Nothing is so obliging as to hold us.

Pascal continues by saying that man in this situation is himself the most complex thing in nature, a monster, a mystery.

This mystery belongs to a completely different category than do scientific problems. Scientific problems can at least eventually be solved in principle, but a mystery is essentially insoluble. In this sense man is a being of enduring mystery (K. Rahner). He not only has questions but is himself a question to which he has ultimately no answer. This clinging mystery is not a kind of irrational holdover; it is the presupposition of rationality. Man thus reposes, precisely in his rationality, on something ultimate and final, on the dimension of the holy. Man transcends himself when eternity is at issue (Pascal). For this holy mystery is obviously greater than man, who remains temporal. It eludes every grasp and concept. We can only touch it, as it were, from afar and from the outside. As soon as we try to name it and give it a title, we must immediately be silent and speechless.

We may surmise and hope that the ultimate

reason, which embraces and empowers everything, is not darkness and a headlong fall into the
yawning void of nothingness, that it is not a void
but fullness, not darkness but a blinding light at
which we cannot now peer because the weak eyes
of our spirit are overwhelmed by it. We can even
advance arguments for this hope. The philosophical
and theological tradition has always tried to give
such arguments in its proofs for God. They are
still possible today if the word *proof* is not understood in the narrow sense that is proper only to
mathematics. Arguments of this sort are nonetheless difficult. They imply numerous contrary
questions and objections, and in the end they
remain theoretical and abstract. Still, they are
important with respect to the educated scorners of
religion (Schleiermacher). They perform a rear-
guard action for the faith, so to speak, and show
that it is intellectually possible, but they are unable
to offer positive proof for it. Thus, they can only
clarify the preliminaries to faith and construct
antechambers for faith.

Such antechambers and points of entry to faith
are particularly important in the contemporary
situation. It is a matter of once again preparing the
ground for the question of God in the face of the
obscuring of the horizon for God. It is also important because, whatever may be said in the
following pages about the gracious gift of faith,

faith is also completely and fully a human act, which wants to be situated and accounted for in an intellectually honest way. It is a matter of tearing down all the lofty intellectual edifices that tower against the knowledge of God and of taking captive all thought for Christ (see 2 Cor 10:5).

IV

The Living Act of Faith

Everything that has been said until now has been preliminary. For when the Bible speaks of faith, it does not do so in the form of general philosophical reflections. They are only necessary to such an extent for us today because we have to clear our way laboriously once again to faith. The Bible, however, still lives completely naturally in the world of the religious. When it speaks of faith, it presents no abstract theory but rather relates a concrete history. It is the history of God's revelation and of man's response in either belief or unbelief. For the Bible faith is not a general and vague notion but something very concrete and specific.

The Testimony of Holy Scripture

The history of Abraham, "our father in faith", is especially important. He lived about 1900 B.C. in Ur of Chaldea. All at once the call came to him: Leave your house, your family, your land, the gods that you had until now, for a land that I,

God, will show you (see Gen 12:1). Abraham did not know this land at all, but he cast himself completely on God's promise and set out on his way. So he, the nomad, became a nomad of faith. God's demands went still further. God promised him numerous descendants, as numerous as the grains of sand on the seashore (see Gen 12:2). But God gave Abraham's wife, Sarah, no son. Who could be surprised that Abraham protested once (see Gen 15:2) and that Sarah simply laughed quietly to herself (see Gen 18:12)? But Abraham hoped against all hope. The Old Testament merely says: "Abraham believed the Lord, and the Lord reckoned it to him as righteousness" (Gen 15:6).

What is faith here other than a total self-abandonment to God's promise and call, a letting go of all human security, a holding to and a standing fast in God's word alone? Faith here is a fundamental decision, which results from a conversion away from one's normal attitude and one's normal security, a standing fast independent of all human security, a trust and a confidence in God alone.

What this means concretely not only for the individual but also for the whole people is made clear in another history, which we read in Isaiah 7. The young and still inexperienced King Ahaz found himself politically in a situation from which there was no escape. A coalition of small states had been formed against him in order to force him to march against the empire of the Assyrians. What was left for Ahaz to do than either to give in to this politically and militarily utterly unreasonable demand or to turn for help to the Assyrians, subjecting himself to them freely and thus giving up Israel's existence as the people of God, with all the consequences both political and religious that would follow? It is understandable that the heart of the King and of the people trembled as the trees of the woods tremble in the wind.

In the midst of this dilemma the prophet Isaiah met the King on the Fuller's Field road. Isaiah hurled at Ahaz only this one thing: "If you do not have faith, you shall not remain" (Is 7:9). For this prophet, who was not really apolitically minded, such faith was no substitute for a reasonable and responsible politics; for him all politics was ultimately unreasonable and irresponsible if it disregarded God and his plan for the sake of immediate and short-term opportunistic considerations. Even in the public domain, faith alone provided the firmest support.

Thus faith as it is understood in the Old Testament means a holding fast to and an acquiring confidence in God, which banishes all anxiety and so makes possible reasonable behavior. "Whoever has faith will not waver" (Is 28:16). Whoever has faith knows: "Your salvation lies in conversion

and peace; only quiet and trust give you strength"
(Is 30:15). Habakkuk puts all of this together when
he says that the righteous person stays alive because
of his faith (see Hab 2:4). According to the biblical
understanding, faith is the basic act and, indeed,
the basic condition of man before God, his fundamental stand and support in God, his life before,
from and in God. Faith of this sort expresses itself
in radical conversion, in confidence and patience,
in inner calm and inner peace, in freedom and
righteousness. Faith of this sort, for which God is
the support and the substance, is the life of man.

In his work entitled *Two Forms of Faith*, Martin
Buber sought to contrast this Old Testament understanding of faith with its New Testament counter-
part. He proposed the thesis that in the Old Testament faith is a confidence in God that touches
upon a man's whole being, whereas in the New
Testament it becomes a mere affirmation of the
truth. From the word *believe*, used in an absolute
way, there is a development to *believing in*.

As a matter of fact, belief in the New Testament
is essentially "belief in Jesus Christ". Nonetheless,
Old and New Testament scholars today are largely
in agreement that Buber's distinction is incorrect.
For even the confidence-faith of the Old Testament
presupposes a listening to God and an acceptance
of his message and his promise. Already in different
places in Genesis and Exodus are to be found what

Buber calls "belief that" (see Gen 45:26; Ex 1:5, 8, 9, 31). By the same token, the New Testament and especially Jesus himself, as well as Paul, also naturally know of faith as an all-embracing stance for the Christian, which affects one's existence and one's life. We encounter this all-embracing understanding of faith particularly in the Gospel miracle stories: "Only believe" (Mk 5:34) and: "Your faith has saved you" (Mk 5:36).

This faith, seen as a basic attitude, is really possible only as a response to the experience of the fidelity, the mercy and the love of God, as it has been revealed to us comprehensively and ultimately in Jesus Christ and in his life, death and Resurrection. Thus faith that is seen as act is sustained and made possible by revelation and its content. Faith seen as act presupposes and includes faith in Jesus Christ. The act of faith and the content of faith are thus inextricably bound together for both the Old and the New Testaments.

The Unity of the Act of Faith and the Content of Faith

By reason of what has been said up until this point, we can now state that faith is as little a contentless belief or a belief that is indifferent to possible content as it is a mere affirmation of texts or dogmas. For the New Testament it is the decisive and all-determining approach to the God who has revealed himself in Jesus Christ with finality as the God of mankind. For John in particular the knowledge of God and of Jesus Christ is a constitutive element of true faith. In the fourth Gospel believing and accepting Christ and coming to Jesus are synonymous expressions (see Jn 5:40; 6:35, 37, 44–45, 65; 7:37). In other New Testament writings the word *faith* is intentionally used in the context of early Christian mission terminology. *Faith* here is a technical word for the response to the proclamation of the Gospel; it comes from hearing and is therefore obedience to the word of proclamation as the good news of God's redemptive deed in Jesus Christ (see Rom 10:17). Already in the later New Testament faith can be seen as teaching. Indeed, as such it is transmitted in clear formulas, and included with these formulas is the warning to hold fast to what has been handed down once for all. With this the path is open to this sort of usage by the early Fathers and the early Councils; by *pistis* or faith they mean the Church's proclamation of the faith and her teaching of the faith.

In the Letter to the Hebrews the New Testament brings both aspects together—the personal, act-oriented aspect of standing fast in God-directed hope and the knowing and being convinced of invisible and inascertainable realities: "But faith is

confidence in what is hoped for and being convinced of things that are not seen" (Heb 11:1).

It was reserved to Saint Augustine to give a
clear explanation of the multileveled biblical data.
Augustine distinguishes a twofold use of the concept of faith, differentiating between the content
of faith (*fides quae creditur*) and the act of faith (*fides
qua creditur*). This distinction was fundamental for
all of the later tradition. It must not be conceived
as a division. Faith is at once both act and content.
The content is only possessed as something carried
out in life; this thing carried out in life, on the
other hand, is always related to the content and
borne and ensouled by the content. The act of faith
and the content of faith constitute an indivisible
whole. This is also taught by the Second Vatican
Council when it describes faith as a total personal
self-surrender (which is the act of faith) to the God
who reveals himself in word and deed and who is
summed up in Jesus Christ (which is the content
of faith).

This has far-reaching significance for today's
problems in passing on the faith. It makes it clear
once again that the real problem is deeper than the
often dismaying lack of knowledge of the content
of the faith. Knowledge of the faith and knowledge
of the catechism are, precisely in the present-day
situation, by no means to be scorned or neglected.
But they can only be suitably passed on and received

when the basic attitudes of faith have successfully been reawakened.

Basic Attitudes of Faith

Let us then first consider the act of faith in detail. In Scholasticism and Neoscholasticism there was a long and bitter dispute over whether faith was an act of the intellect or of the will. Most Neoscholastics, in agreement with Thomas Aquinas, saw faith primarily as an act of the intellect. Correspondingly, faith was viewed primarily as an affirmation of the truth. Neoprotestantism was different; it and in particular Schleiermacher saw faith as an act of feeling. The Catholic Modernists seized upon this notion. Today it remains an issue to the extent that an accent is placed one-sidedly on the personal experience of faith. From the point of view of the Bible, all of the solutions that have been mentioned are one-sided. For the Bible faith is an act of the whole person. It is neither a merely intellectual affirmation of the truths of the faith nor a simple decision of the will, and it is certainly not just a feeling devoid of content. In the act of faith all the powers of the soul—intellect, will and feeling—come together. The act of faith is a total attitude that encompasses all these human powers.

58

It means holding fast to God and grounding one's whole existence in God.

The first basic attitude of faith is listening and becoming aware, opening oneself and being receptive. Faith cannot be created and produced; one must become aware of it and be receptive to it. Only a person who is open and who opens himself to what is totally other and to the newness of the divine mystery, only a person who is not simply ready with his own views and opinions, can come to faith. Thus faith is, secondly, bound up with the reversal of the ordinary ways of doing and seeing things. There is no faith without the letting go of old certitudes, without reversal and conversion. This can be a very painful process; it can mean saying good-bye to familiar ideas and being ready for contradiction and conflict. Whoever believes marches to a different drummer and does not follow the crowd. Along with this there belongs to faith, in the third place, an attitude of hope, a courageous stretching out of oneself to the new. Faith is thus a way that must be traversed, a holding fast to and a grounding oneself in what is not yet possessed. It is the courage of the person who goes after a thing in its entirety and in so doing contradicts the narrow-minded philistine.

Such a reversal of self and such self-abandonment to God and his word are, in the fourth place, only possible in the act of trust. The first word of faith is consequently not "I believe that" but rather "I believe you". The love of God that has been accepted in trust can be responded to by the believer in no other way than by love. Faith is, in a manner of speaking, a declaration of love for God. God's turning toward us, therefore, leads of necessity to our turning toward God. And so prayer is the most important form of expression that faith takes. Indeed, without prayer faith evaporates; a faith without prayer is not possible.

Love, fifthly, leads inexorably to action. Because the believer knows that he is accepted by God, he can also accept himself, others and the world anew. It is in this sense that Scripture says that faith without works is dead (see James 2:17). Faith may thus not remain lip service; it must be maintained in concrete service for one's neighbor; it must bring forth the fruits of the Spirit—love, joy, peace, patience, kindness, goodness, trustfulness, mildness and self-control (see Gal 5:22–23). The believer must commit himself to the dignity of man, to justice, liberty and peace; he must, to the extent possible, transform his life and the world. Finally, faith is not action and certainly not activism, but rather calm and peace in God. It keeps itself in patience and self-possession. It can, to recall Paul and Ignatius of Loyola, accommodate itself to anything. Its only concern is that God be glorified in everything.

Faith as Way

Many Christians have a hard time nowadays with such descriptions of Christian faith. They very often experience their faith as a questioning and seeking, and they have difficulties with many truths of the faith. They are besieged by questions, which color all of life and reality for them. Seeking and questioning of this sort, if they are humbly open to the knowledge of the truth, should not be confused with an arbitrary and stiff-necked rejection or with an irresolute putting off of a decision about faith, which is real doubt with regard to faith. Acquiescent halfheartedness concerning recognized truth is certainly reprehensible. But that is fundamentally distinct from being questioning and open with respect to knowledge or to full knowledge of the truth.

Honest and conscientious seeking of the truth is in fact an inner possibility of faith. Faith, after all, is part of the human pilgrimage, and it is turned toward the infinite God. This excludes every self-assured and arrogant closing off of oneself to questions and problems as being directed against the inner dynamic of the faith. Such would not be a perfect faith but rather a perverted form of true faith, an unwillingness to learn and a lack of openness to the infinite mystery of God. Thus faith is not a fixed and immovable standpoint but a way. There is not only a way to faith, therefore, but also a way within faith itself. Even in faith the law of progress holds.

The Apostle Paul speaks of a growth in faith (see 2 Cor 10:15). Faith is governed by the rule of every living thing: it wants to grow. Standing still is for faith, too, a step backward, which leads to its stunting and finally to its dying out. Therefore, the masters of the spiritual life have always given advice from out of the treasure of their own experience of faith as to how it can be protected and cultivated, so that it may strike deeper roots and produce rich fruit.

Certainly the study of the faith belongs to its growth, particularly reading and meditating on Holy Scripture. What is not known cannot be loved. By the same token, a deepened knowledge of the riches of faith will strengthen one's joy in the faith and one's joy in believing. It will also help in meeting objections to the faith and in not becoming unsettled by them. Thus it is not an uninformed and blind faith that is the ideal but rather an informed and educated faith. Indeed, it is faith itself that seeks understanding and that strives for deeper insight into what is believed.

The practice of the faith, its conscious translation into life, contributes still more to its firming up and to its growth. Previously it used to be recommended that the act of faith be regularly awakened and consciously made. Where such a remembering and interiorizing do not take place, faith slumbers and eventually dies out. Therefore, faith needs times and places for quiet and reflection, but it also needs a certain regularity and order. The self-expression of faith does not occur only in silence and within the heart; it occurs also in speaking and in dialogue with others as well as in witnessing to the faith before others. Only in speech and expression do our thoughts and decisions take on their definitive form, and only in the acting out of faith does this form become secure.

Finally, there is no life, and certainly no growth in faith, without recourse to God and without speaking to him in both private and public prayer. Inasmuch as the act of faith is ultimately directed utterly to God alone, prayer is really the soul and the breath of faith. Without prayer faith lacks nourishment; without prayer it suffers from lack of fresh air, so that it suffocates. Hence in prayer we have to ask again and again for the gift and the power of the Holy Spirit himself. For ultimately faith, like growth in faith, is pure gift and pure grace.

Many saints have described this way of faith exhaustively. In so doing they have made it clear that this is no broad and easy street but a narrow and steep way (see Mt 7:13–14). It is a way of purification and of constant conversion, of often painful farewells and courageous new beginnings. In the unanimous experience of the saints, this way will also always lead through the desert of inner aridity. Whoever looks only for sensible consolation is too dependent on himself and has not yet found the selflessness of love, which is rooted in faith. Indeed, the experience of the desert is fundamental to growth in faith. The way within faith, in the end, is a way in patience and in daily fidelity. Extraordinary experiences may happen from time to time, but the truly extraordinary consists in doing the ordinary with extraordinary fidelity. Only thus are a slow ascent and an ever-deeper insight and enlightenment in faith possible, until inner calm and inner peace in God are attained.

Such faith, in hope and love, is a long, lifelong, way. It is the way of the imitation of Jesus Christ, which is at the same time the all-embracing content of faith.

V

The Truth of Faith

However beautiful everything that has been said about Christian faith may sound, it is as nothing if we do not also give an account to ourselves of the reason for our faith. That is how the question is intended: What is our faith founded upon? What is it built upon? What gives it its certitude? How, then, can we give an account of our hope—an account to ourselves and to others (see 1 Pet 3:15)? How is the truth of Christian faith to be explained?

God's Revealed Truth
as the Basis of Faith

Such an account implies a common basis for agreement. But what else can such a basis be and what else is common to everyone besides our human reason? As we have seen, it is presupposed in faith. For modern rationalism, human reason is not just a receptive faculty and, to that extent, a presupposition for faith; much more than that, it is also the horizon, the framework and, indeed, the criterion for the knowledge of the faith. Consequently, for rationalism, unlike for the Christian tradition, the faith must be reasonable; it must justify itself to reason and be placed on a reasonable basis. This comes down to a "religion within the bounds of reason alone" (Kant). In our century the intellectualistic limits of this position have been split asunder. Its line of argument, however, is still utilized. This is particularly the case when statements of faith are only accepted inasmuch as or because they fit into a previously established anthropological or sociological scheme, or else because they are useful either as a means to peace and order or as a catalyst for world change.

Such a basis for faith actually does away with the fundamental attitude for faith. In faith we do not continue to rely in high-minded fashion on our own human insight, our human judgments and concerns. Faith means, as we have said, trusting and confiding in God. Whoever believes abandons his human certitudes and security; he sets up something that is outside of himself and that is infinitely more certain than all our human certitudes. The ultimate basis for faith is God himself, his revealed truth and fidelity; his reliability is the reliability of our faith. It is not for nothing that the Hebrew word for believe is *aman*, which means to be firm, sure, certain. We know this word even today in the Amen of liturgical language. To believe, we could say, thus means to say Amen to God, with all its consequences (G. Ebeling).

The First Vatican Council therefore declared in opposition to rationalism that we believe that what has been revealed by God is true "not because we have seen the inner truth of things through the natural light of reason but rather on the authority of the revealing God himself". The revealed truth of God is, according to this, the ultimate basis for faith. The certitude of faith that is grounded on God and not on human reason is in fact not less than that of knowledge; it is, instead, much greater; it is, as the theological tradition says, more firmly established than anything else. "In you, O Lord, I have hoped; I shall never be ashamed."

But the theological problem is still by no means solved with the biblical and dogmatic thesis that God himself is the basis of faith. On the contrary, it is only posed with what has been said. The question is, namely, how we become aware of God's truth. Are we not, with the biblical and dogmatic assertion that has been made, moving in a circle? Are we not, in other words, presupposing in this assertion what must first be established? For when we say that God is the basis of faith in God, it is an assertion of this sort and is indeed the very content of faith. Is faith, in the end, its own basis?

The Eyes of Faith

Augustine himself struggled with this problem. The difficulty, he said, was so great that only God could solve it, and God solves it by giving us faith. We could not even, as Augustine indicates, seek for faith if God did not come to the aid of our search. This answer seems at first like an embarrassed solution: one has the impression that God is appearing on the scene in *deus ex machina* fashion.

Actually Augustine's argument is not quite as naive as it looks at first. For an ultimate basis, which is under discussion here, can in fact never be established on a yet more ultimate basis. If, then, I believe in God as the ultimate basis of all reality, then this faith can itself never be grounded in anything higher. The alternative placed before us, therefore, is whether a man himself can give himself an ultimate basis or whether he will bow down before an ultimate and absolute basis, which can only be God, and acknowledge him. If he does this latter, it is because God, who is the truth and hence the light of life, has dawned on him.

The acknowledgment of God is thus no blind groping. Rather it is enlightened by the light of God's truth, which shines upon man. It is in this

sense that Augustine and the whole tradition speak
of the light of faith and of the grace of faith
enlightening man. Again and again they cite the
verse of the Psalm: "In your light we see light"
(Ps 36:9). P. Rousselot has spoken of the eyes of
faith enlightened by the light of grace.

This answer is biblically well founded. Jesus
himself makes clear that "those who are without"
hear his parables, to be sure, but they do not
understand. To the disciples, however, the mystery
of the kingdom of God is "given" (Mk 4:11).
Therefore Peter is told after having confessed Jesus
as the Messiah and the Son of God: "Flesh and
blood have not revealed this to you, but my Father
in heaven" (Mt 16:17). According to Paul, no eye
has seen and no ear heard what God has prepared
for those who love him, but the Spirit of God,
who sounds the deep things of God, reveals it to
our spirit. Thus only the spiritual person can judge
all things (see 1 Cor 2:9–10, 15). The letter to the
Ephesians speaks of the enlightened eyes of the
heart (see Eph 1:18), and the Gospel of John says
succinctly: "No one can come to me unless the
Father, who sent me, draw him" (Jn 6:44).

God himself thus shows himself as "drawing"
in faith, as fascinating and convincing. In faith
there dawns on man a light, so to say, in which
everything else can be seen anew, better and more
profoundly. To the extent that faith is a unique

experience of revelation, it is the gift of a new possibility of sight that contains its evidence in itself.

An Analysis of Faith?

But the questioning is still not over with these answers. If it is true that the certitude of faith as an ultimate certitude cannot be derived from some still higher certitude, and if it is thus true that God as the truth and the basis of faith can only become evident through himself, then yet another question is raised: How do we become aware of this bright and illuminating light of truth? How does the believer lay immediate hold of the truth of God as the ultimate basis of his faith?

The posing of this question is called the analysis of faith because it analyzes the act of faith on its deepest level. The theologians of the seventeenth to the nineteenth centuries in particular offered the most subtle arguments relative to these questions, but they came to no single result that was universally satisfying. On the contrary, Kleutgen called this "the cross and the torture of theologians". Certainly it is one of the most difficult questions in all of theology; it is *the* fundamental problem of theology.

We do not wish to, nor can we, treat all the

subtle and refined answers of the theologians of the period just mentioned and go into the scholastic distinctions between Suarez, de Lugo, Billot and others. They are not completely satisfying and persuasive anyhow, for they run the danger of turning the decision to believe into the outcome of a kind of logical syllogism. But that is impossible from the very start, since what is at issue here is an ultimate presupposition. Here lies the limit of every purely logical analysis of faith. Hence theology in general today goes back to Thomas Aquinas and seeks to continue along the lines that he established.

The Person Who Believes Sees More

Thomas begins by saying that man, fundamentally and by nature, seeks God. Man inquires, as we have seen, about the whole of reality and about its ultimate basis and goal. Thus, in every act of knowledge and desire he touches upon God as the basis and goal of all of reality. He has, to be sure, only a global and unclear knowledge of this; he can never fully conceptualize this vague hint. And so he is always unsatisfied; he possesses an insatiable dynamism that is constantly yearning. He is only fulfilled when he meets God face to face in an eternal vision. This is the sum total of human fulfillment. Faith in God is, according to Thomas, a certain anticipation of this goal. In it the person has already set himself upon the road to God and clings to him by love. This foretaste does not occur in such a way as to be immediately face to face, but it is mediated by an external revelation.

In the external signs of revelation natural reason can recognize traces, indications, points of reference for faith or, as used to be said, appropriate reasons for believing. But natural knowledge is in fact insufficient to perceive God's revelations with ultimate certitude in these things. For this there is need of a connatural means of perceiving the divine reality, and this is the light of faith. But with the eyes of faith we can recognize God's truth with certitude in the external forms of revelation.

Man hopes in the truth that is God with, so to say, every fiber of his being. This is what he is on the watch for, without ever being able to reach it by himself. The light of faith, which permits us to recognize God's truth in the external forms of revelation, is consequently the ultimate truth over us. It is nothing foreign to us, no external addition to the light of reason, but rather its ultimate fulfillment; it is the salvation of mankind. The shining light of God is not a darkening of reason but rather, on the contrary, its enlightenment. The light of grace is connected with the natural search for God, with the innate idea of God that men have, so as to bring it to its fulfillment, completion and determination, which is impossible to accomplish by the powers of reason alone. Thus the truth of God dawns upon man intuitively, so to speak, as the truth that is above him, in an enlightening, convincing and compelling way.

More recent theology has linked itself to this genial teaching of Thomas Aquinas. At the same time, often in connection with Cardinal Newman's *Grammar of Assent*, it brings it further. Newman began early in his career by saying that in mathematics, to be sure, we are led to certitude by strict argumentation but that in life we are guided by probability. Thus the individual appropriate reasons for believing the faith are not proofs; even their multiplication and their convergence do not provide logical certitude. But they give, nonetheless, a probability and an intellectual security, on the basis of which a decision to believe is humanly possible, intellectually responsible and morally binding. But there is a question of real, absolute certitude regarding the faith only when these converging arguments are considered in the grace-filled light of faith.

Newman clarified this thesis through numerous comparisons. He used, for example, the work of an archaeologist, who has at first only individual findings from ruins, coins, inscriptions and perhaps a few relevant literary testimonies. On the basis of what are often as few witnesses as these, he reconstructs, not without using his intuition and imagination, a complete edifice, and indeed sometimes a whole cultural epoch. Only intuition of this sort permits the individual findings to be understood in any real way. Newman also adduced medical diagnosis as an example. At first a doctor sees only a few symptoms of disease, but thanks to his medical "eye" he recognizes in these symptoms the causes of the disease. From these, again, the symptoms are clear to him. The beautiful phrase of Thomas Aquinas is apropos in this regard: "Where love is, there is an eye." True love does not blind but gives vision; it first embraces another person in his credibility and goodness. The same is true of the light of faith; it first permits us to appreciate reality in all its breadth and depth.

Only Love Is Believable

Hans Urs von Balthasar goes an essential step beyond what has already been said. In his voluminous work *The Glory of the Lord*, he develops a complete Christian teaching on perception. He shows that the light of faith and the grace of faith do not need to be imagined as something that flows "directly from above" into the believer and enlightens him independently of the content of faith or in addition to the content of faith. Rather the object of faith, who is Jesus Christ, brings with himself the light and the understanding by which he can be recognized by the believer. In Jesus Christ and in his proclamation the light of faith streams through the Church. The Apostle Paul says that we are enlightened by the knowledge of God's glory in the face of Christ (see 2 Cor 4:6). Jesus Christ bears witness to himself and imposes himself. Therefore von Balthasar speaks not of subjective but of objective evidence. It is the evidence of the form of revelation itself.

Von Balthasar expresses his solution with this formula: "Only love is believable." Love cannot be proven; it makes itself credible. It is thus that the love of God, which appeared in Jesus Christ, convinces man and gives him a certitude of a particular sort. Christ is mediated to us concretely in the Church, in her word and in her sacraments (the liturgy) and, what is especially important for von Balthasar, in the representatives of the Church. These are not primarily the official representatives but rather the saints. In them the light and the love of God gleam in the world. They give credibility to the proclamation of the faith; they are convincing. For love is the meaning of being.

What, then, are the basis and the truth of faith? Something that transcends all knowledge and yet enlightens all knowledge, giving it breadth and depth and perspective—the light that was already shining from the very beginning of creation in the world and that has finally burst forth in Jesus Christ, who is God's revealed love itself (see Jn 1:1–14). Only this, ultimately, is convincing. This is the truth that makes us free (see Jn 8:32).

VI

The Power of
Faith to Open up
and Transform Reality

Whoever wishes to know must have faith. We have proceeded from this basic conviction of Origen and Augustine, which is once again apropos today. It means that the person who believes sees more. True faith, like true love, gives sight and does not make blind. Now it is a matter not only of asserting and establishing this thesis in a formal way but also of verifying it materially and from the point of view of content. The question to which we turn is: What lets faith see? How does it open up reality for us? What is the reality that is embraced in faith?

In asking this, we are not concerning ourselves with a dogmatic investigation of the particular content of faith. We are not really posing a dogmatic question but, in a certain fashion, a fundamental theological one. We are not asking about the reality of faith in itself but about faith's power to open up reality. In this we are limiting ourselves to three aspects—the world as creation, the problem of evil and the message of redemption.

The World as Creation

If the distinctive mark of the Christian faith consists in the fact that it not only implies the general belief that life has a meaning but also, and beyond this, names God as the basis of this belief, then this in turn implies the understanding that reality is created. For creation means that the world has the ultimate basis of its being, and of its being this way rather than some other way, in God.

Christian thought on creation has been and is now one of the great points of contention in the discussion between faith and science. The trial of Galileo and the controversy over the theory of evolution of Darwin and his successors have had their effects to this day. They have led to a schism that does not exist among believers but that is evident between faith and the modern world. To be sure, theologians and, along with them, most preachers have learned in the meantime that the Bible is not a textbook; it does not teach us what the heavens are like but rather, as Galileo said, how to get to heaven. Consequently a distinction must be made between the time-conditioned form and the enduring substance of the biblical creation

accounts. Most theologians today see no fundamental difference any longer between faith in
creation and an evolutionary doctrine that is aware
of its limitations. But the centuries-old disputes
have left behind their traces and wounds within
the Church. They have also made many preachers
suspicious of the teaching on creation. There is
astonishingly little talk of it in preaching and theology, and when there is, it is often halfhearted,
tortured and almost apologetic.

But what is a faith in God that has nothing more
to say of reality in general, that withdraws into an
existential relationship with God, into trust in
God, and in this interiority if it forgets the exterior
world of the cosmos, pushes it aside or gives it up?
Can God still be God—that is, the all-embracing
and all-determining reality—if the world is no
longer God's world? Must not a worldless God
necessarily lead to a Godless world? If God no
longer has anything to do with the world and with
the worldly concerns of men, then we must not be
surprised if men no longer want to have anything
to do with God and encounter our message without any interest. A theology of salvation history
and an existential understanding of the faith that
leave out the connection with the reality of creation
become a gnosis that is defenseless in the face of
the accusation of projection and illusion that is
part of the critique of religion.

The neglect of the creation accounts is particularly incomprehensible in view of the fact that the stock of the teaching on creation stands remarkably high at the moment. For the theory of evolution, when its scientific theoretical status is judged, can never be an alternative to or a substitute for faith in creation. It always presupposes something that is becoming and that is inquiring about the "how" of becoming. It does not explain the "that" of being and is not an answer to the question: Why does something exist at all? Still less than to the question about the basis of being does it respond to the question about the meaning of being: What is anything for? What is everything for? What am I for? These are precisely the questions that the doctrine of evolution and every purely scientific explanation of the world never reach and that the message of creation responds to.

The answer to this is as urgently necessary today as it ever was. Today, in fact, it carries a completely new urgency. Man's threat to everything living has again aroused a sense of reverence for what exists and a responsibility for the condition of reality. It has again awakened understanding with regard to the fact that there will be a catastrophe if the world is seen and treated exclusively as a hominized world, as a world of man and as material for man. The world as creation, however, means that as God's world it is indeed a world *for* man but not simply a world *of* man. It is not the product of man but was given to him by God and was therefore given to him to act responsibly toward. Thus it has a depth, a mystery, a dignity that man must respect. It was also created, to be sure, for his use and enjoyment, but it serves still more for the praise of the Creator, in which man may and should join.

What follows from this view of reality as created? I limit myself to just two points:

1. *The Logos-relatedness and reasonableness of the world.* The biblical accounts of creation need only be compared once with the creation myths of the rest of the world of the time in order for one to see the vast differences between them. In the latter the cosmos results from bloody battles among the gods or among the demonic giants of a primordial epoch. The whole strange experience of man with the world and with himself, the experience of the unfathomable and of the demonic elements of reality is mirrored in stories such as these. The Bible is utterly different. Reality has its source and foundation in God's free creative word alone. It is created by and through his Logos, and therefore it is marked by the Logos. It is an expression of God's wisdom, ordered according to "measure, number and weight" (Wis 11:20). The creation account thus shows itself as truly enlightened and as supportive of the reasonableness of creation.

Later on, the Church's teaching time and time
again defended the reality of creation and vin-
dicated it against the disparaging accusation that it
was bad. More than that: because the world comes
from God's Logos and is created according to his
idea, it is not irrational matter but rather stamped
with the spiritual; consequently, it is very accessible
to our own spirit and intellectually knowable.

How can the knowableness of the world and the
ability to formulate its arrangement in laws of
nature be explained except by saying that it is
analogous to the intellect? But how can that be,
since it is not of our own doing, apart from a
creating intellect? Natural scientists like Kepler
and Einstein knew of these interconnections and
understood their natural science in the context of
an amazed reflection on the very order of the
world. Its derivation from some eternal matter, in
contrast, explains nothing at all inasmuch as this
matter cannot explain itself. Moreover, this is a
scientific fable today because the concept of matter
has fallen apart in the wake of the theory of relativity
and the quantum theory, and no one can say
anymore exactly what matter really is. Jacques
Monod, who rejects as unscientific every theological consideration and hence, obviously, the
idea of God, and who explains the whole world
from an interplay of chance and necessity, himself
recounts what François Mauriac said after he had

attended a lecture by Monod on the subject: "What this professor wants to inflict on us is far more unbelievable than what we poor Christians were ever expected to believe." Monod himself cannot help but describe his explanation as absurd. But in the meantime here too the discussion has proceeded further. In biochemistry as well as in physics the talk is all of structures, cycles, rules and so forth, quite apart from the philosophical attempts to demonstrate that purely causal explanations are totally insufficient and that, instead, they presuppose teleological explanations—and, indeed, that they are themselves teleological explanations in disguise.

As Christians today we have every reason to defend the reasonableness of reality, in order thus to check the irrational thinking of the self-interested and power-hungry groups, the ideologies of violence and the enthusiastic utopias that endanger mankind, and to work toward objective, reasonable solutions to problems and conflicts. As the representatives of faith in creation we are today the truly enlightened ones.

2. *Freedom and the Sabbath-structure of creation.* It is a basic assertion of faith that God created the world freely and out of pure love, without any external or internal compulsion, because he wished his creatures to participate in his being and his life. But if the world is a work of freedom, then it is

also a world of freedom—that is, a world that is not determined by blind forces. If it were, then there would be no room in it for human freedom. Then men, with their questions, longings, needs and worries, would be camped like gypsies on the outskirts of a cosmos that would be oblivious of them; then the situation of man in the world would be absurd. Only if creation comes from freedom and is stamped with freedom is freedom possible and can the free person live meaningfully and have an effect in the world. But if it comes from freedom and is oriented to freedom, then rules and structures that make freedom possible must also exist in the world; then there must be free room of every sort for individuals as well as for culture, science and, not least of all, for religion and its unhindered, free, public practice.

This thought can go a step further. Because the world comes from God's freedom and has been designed for human freedom, it cannot just be a world of work. Human work is the expression and the elaboration of human freedom; correctly understood, it is not slavery but the expression of human domination. Therefore there is also a human right to work. The creation account, however, concludes ultimately not with the human task of domination but with that of worship, with the Sabbath. The world has a Sabbath-structure; it is oriented to rest, to peace and to the glorification of God. Thus human freedom does not blossom when men are preoccupied with using and enjoying worldly possessions. It is ultimately goalless and finds its fulfillment in what is goalless—in play, leisure, art, feasts and celebrations. Man is not merely a worker; he is also a player. He is ultimately a prayer and adorer. He is not the slave of work but, rather, called to the freedom of the children of God. It is not without reason that the Eucharist is the center of Christian existence.

The glorification of God is at once the salvation of man and of the world. Already in the Old Testament, the Sabbath is celebrated as a boon, and Jesus places its original meaning once again in the foreground when he says: "The Sabbath is for man." Irenaeus of Lyons expresses this in the famous formula: "The glory of God is man fully alive." Irenaeus wanted to make man aware of his true dignity and to point out the meaning of his posture, which is upright and elevated above other things. In our overplanned and excessively goal-oriented world the liturgy is free space, pure and simple. Here man can find peace, and here he can breathe easily. Hence the selfish and profiteering attacks on Sundays and holidays must be resisted for the sake of mankind. Hence precisely today the celebration of the liturgy is the decisive service offered to man.

Faith in creation is thus something utterly different from a dusty relic of an out-of-date world view. It is the meaning of the world and the transformation of the world all in one. We need it precisely today. But there is an objection that we have to make: Is not this creation-oriented view of the world too idealistic and optimistic? Is it realistic enough to hold its ground against the "really real"? We are confronted here with the problem of evil.

The Problem of Evil

Our approach to the problem of evil nowadays is discordant. On the one hand we experience the danger and the insecurity of our reality as hardly ever before; terror and violence are commonplace. In social and international discussions there reigns a downright pharisaical pathos characterized by moralizing complaints and finger pointing. On the other hand we have found a thousand explanations and sociological and psychological theories to help us avoid the frightfulness of reality: evil is shown to be a by-product of evolution, an illusion or a complex, the result of structures, and so on. When it is actually a question of guilt, we always find it elsewhere, in structures, relationships, nature and the past. An uncanny defense mechanism and a remarkable craze of guilt-lessness are in play, and with their help we steal away from our responsibility. Guilt and sin are themes that are pushed to one side, even in preaching. People prefer to speak of deviant be-havior and to relegate this to statistics, where everything can be reversed: what is deviant today can be the rule tomorrow. The thing that is im-periled here is nothing less than man himself, the freedom and responsibility of man, the truth about his real situation.

The Christian message of sin, of the unsaved condition of man and of his need to be redeemed seek to confront us, precisely in this situation of ours, with the complete and unadorned truth about our life. In many respects it uses the mythical language of images and symbols. But the depths of reality cannot be put into language without employing images and symbols. Mythical images and symbols are not childish fancies but indications of reality. When they are not viewed simplistically, they do complete justice to the manifold and diverse experiences of man. And so the Christian response to the old and ever-new human question of the origin of evil is not as simple as it is usually por-trayed by Christianity's adversaries. It is threefold.

Scripture and tradition speak, first, about the personal sin of the individual. It is I who am guilty, and not structures, establishments or other kinds of mechanisms. "You are the man" (2 Sam 12:7). "Against you alone have I sinned" (Ps 51:4). Out of this speak the honesty and the courage to stand by oneself and one's deeds and to take responsibility for them. Out of this speaks the understanding of man as a person, who is more than a composite of functions and more than the ensemble of his societal relationships.

The individual person exists only as a person in a context; the individual man exists only as a man in a context. He is a social being who is bound up in the whole of a family, a society and humanity in general. The individual determines the style, the spirit, the atmosphere of the whole, but he is likewise determined by the whole, both for good and for ill. In this respect other men are not merely a good or a bad example; they are a piece of myself and they determine me in what I am. The Christian teaching on original sin intends to articulate this ontological involvement in the distancing from God and in the evil that characterizes this shared sinfulness. It intends, thereby, to destroy at the same time the illusion of an unbroken world in which we think that we are able to take refuge. It also tells us, however, that we must be careful with concrete indications of personal guilt, that we may not judge rashly and prejudge. Hence there are, in an analogical sense, structural contexts of evil; there are conditions that arise out of sin and that provide an occasion for and an incentive to evil. Wherever possible, the Church must offer a prophetic critique of such unjust structures and call injustice, violence and oppression by their names. Wherever possible, we must act against these things with all our strength. Yet we must and we should know that we cannot catapult ourselves out of the common condition of humanity, that we cannot redeem ourselves.

Finally, Christian teaching knows of still a third dimension with which we today have the greatest difficulty and about which we ought to speak only with caution. Not to speak of this, however, would run counter to the clear witness of the New Testament, which lays great emphasis in many passages on the devil, Satan, demons and wicked powers and forces. Silence in this regard would also not do justice to human experience. Man is not only bound up in the web of humanity; he is also rooted in the cosmos, with all its darkness. The devil used to be popularly portrayed as harmless. Today we have every reason to reflect more deeply on "the mystery of evil" (2 Th 2:7) in order to do justice both to the testimony of Scripture and to the monstrous wickedness that indisputably exists in the world.

Christian teaching demonstrates its realism in that it does not derive these three facts from one another. Societal evil is not only an accumulation and an extrapolation of individual guilt; neither are the devil or original sin alibis for personal responsibility. Evil is self-contradictory and therefore cannot be reduced to a single factor!

But one thing is common to all three facts: they exist beyond the alternative of dualism and monism. The assertions that derive from them insist that reality itself is not evil, that it is good. In addition, there is no eternal contest between good and evil; God is the Lord of all reality. Yet Christianity neither represents a cheap monistic optimism and faith in progress, whether this be idealistic or materialistic, nor justifies a fundamentally dualistic pessimism. Christian faith knows about the entanglements from which no individualism, no people, no class or race can free itself. Whenever we attempt to shake off in revolutionary fashion the burden of history, even this new beginning is conditioned by the past. Violence has to be used to resist violence. Thus it is that injustice and new suffering, new bitterness and new hate are brought along into the better order that has been striven for. One moves in a diabolical circle of guilt and revenge. Every revolution up to the present has been betrayed.

The Christian message is consequently realistic, also, precisely in the fact that it stands beyond the alternative of optimism and pessimism. Neither is

The Power of Faith

it dualism or monism. Reality is, instead, personally structured and designed with a view to the historical meeting of God's freedom and man's response. It is realistic because it takes seriously the reality of the infinitely unique person and his inalienable responsibility for the whole and in the whole. It understands this personal responsibility as a responsibility before God. He alone knows the human heart. For him it is a matter not of judgment but of forgiveness. Only against the backdrop of the message of mercy, grace and forgiveness can one rightly speak in Christian fashion about guilt and sin. Only against this backdrop is this teaching endurable; only then is it even understandable. For only in the face of God's love and goodness do our own wickedness and unkindness dawn on us. The opposite is also true: only in the face of the phenomenon of evil and sin is the message of salvation and redemption realistic and serious. This message may not be cut in half. It becomes pious but emptily soothing talk when people no longer trust themselves to speak of sin and guilt and when they no longer proclaim the message of conversion.

This Christian realism about the person and about the personal orientation of the world is ultimately a realism of hope. Inasmuch as it is a consequence of the goodness of both the Creator and his creation, it knows that the stronger conquers the less strong and that, in the end, good and not evil will bear away the victory. Therefore it is always sensible to do the good and to stand up for it. Christianity takes evil seriously and thereby relativizes it at the same time. It does not submit to it in defeatist fashion but sets up in opposition to it the hope in the infinite reality of God and his redemption. The light that shines on the world from redemption is the only one that can check despair in the face of evil, that acknowledges the ultimately indestructible hope of mankind, that does it justice, that puts fresh heart in it and that brings it to fulfillment.

The Message of Redemption

When Scripture speaks of redemption, it uses numerous images and concepts. It speaks not only negatively of redemption (which we frequently refer to nowadays as liberation, which is also scriptural) but positively as well, in terms of life, grace, peace, freedom, righteousness, reconciliation, healing, friendship and communion with God through Jesus Christ in the Holy Spirit. In our present context we shall not develop this many-faceted and rich message; we shall treat it here only from a particular point of view. We shall ask if and how this central aspect of the Christian proclamation is not a kind of ornament and addition, a merely ideological superstructure, or if and how, rather, it does justice to the reality of man and to his experience.

The theology of our century has pursued this question with great seriousness. De Lubac, K. Rahner and von Balthasar, to name only a few, have overcome the purely external or so-called extrinsic interrelationship of nature and grace that first appeared in the seventeenth and eighteenth centuries and that dominated the Neoscholasticism of the nineteenth and early twentieth centuries. This was far more than an ivory-tower debate. Behind it lay the pastoral awareness of a growing alienation of faith and experience and also of the Church and modern culture. But if the central aspect of faith no longer has anything to do with reality, then it appears to most people as an ideological luxury—good enough to add a little ceremony to particularly significant human events like birth, marriage and death, but unnecessary and useless in a prosaic and hard day-to-day life. The objection, which was certainly taken seriously, to this "new theology" was that in it the gratuitous- ness—the freedom—of grace was no longer fully guaranteed; it had become a necessary supplement to and completion of reality, and thus it was no longer really grace.

Theology has to find its way between the Scylla

of an exclusively external interrelationship and the Charybdis of an internally necessary interrelationship between nature and grace. It does this while holding on to the great and ancient tradition of the Church Fathers and particularly Thomas Aquinas. Along with these theologians of the past it turns away from a one-dimensional, materialistic or idealistic understanding of man. It is realism to the extent that it recalls the multileveled nature and even the paradoxical quality of man.

Man is "a spirit in the world". He is a materially conditioned, mortal and bodily being, and at the same time he is a spirit that, as Aristotle already knew, is "in some way everything". He is open to the world, intentionally related to the whole of reality. Thus it is that man questions and explores everything that is to be met with, everything that is ascertainable. Thoughts are free; for thinking there are no stop signs, for fantasy there are no limits, and the yearning and the hope of man have their goal in the infinite. Since man is, on the one hand, out to get something that can be his "one and all", and since fundamentally he cannot, on the other hand, find this "one and all" in this finite world, he is the only living thing that we know of that can be discontented, disappointed and frustrated —and that often enough is these things. There is a melancholy in fulfillment; every time that one attains one's goal, one senses that it is not what one had really sought. Nothing in the world is big enough to fill the breadth, depth and height of the human heart. Our freedom can only be fulfilled through community and friendship with others' freedom. But even human love is finite; humanly speaking, it finds its limits at last in death. Only a complete freedom, only an infinite, eternal life can fulfill a person. Thus man infinitely transcends man (Pascal). Only God is great enough to lead our heart to inner peace. And so our heart is restless until it rests in God (Augustine).

Hence this is the paradox of man: in himself he goes beyond himself. Characteristically he strives for a completion that he cannot provide for himself. For if he grasped at God and wanted to be like God, then he would be doing violence to God and degrading God to an idol. Then he would become megalomaniacal; he would become a violent tyrant, a "superman", who in reality would be inhuman. Thus man stands between Prometheus and Sisyphus, between megalomaniacal pride and hesitant timidity. Who can help him in this humanly inescapable situation?

The answer, which in the end is the only possible one, is the message of grace. It affirms that the end for which man has been created and to which he has been called, but which he can never attain by his own effort, is given to him by God as a pure gift. Still more, grace is not a "something" that

God gives us; grace is God himself. Grace is God's bestowal of self on and gift of self to men. And so redemption not only takes place from God and through God; redemption is redemption in God; it is the most intimate friendship and communion with him. The divinization of man (to use the terminology of the Fathers) is the true human-ization of man and his deepest fulfillment. The Incarnation of God in Jesus Christ and our par-ticipation in it in the Holy Spirit are therefore the meaning and goal of creation. Jesus Christ, finally, does not only open us to who God is for us; he also opens to us the meaning and goal of man, he opens man to man. Only the person who knows Christ knows man too.

This thesis is directed against a twofold ten-dency. It resists the one-dimensional materialistic-economic view of man and his behavior, which sees happiness in a mere satisfaction of economic needs. This view fails to recognize the supreme value of the human person, whose happiness con-sists not in merely having more but rather in being more. Man is not simply what he eats; he does not live on bread alone; he wants more and is more. The Christian message of grace defends this supreme value. Our thesis is also directed against a second tendency that demands not too little but rather too much of man. This is possible both idealistically and materialistically. According to this view, man is himself supposed to create this supreme value through his own moral, scientific and technical achievements. He is supposed to bring about the kingdom of peace and of freedom either evolutionarily or revolutionarily. For the Bible this would not be a legitimate way of thinking. It demands too much of man, because it ultimately demands of him that he play God. Man lives in this case not out of grace and mercy; he goes down to destruction by way of excessive demands that are graceless and merciless.

The central aspect of the Christian message, which is a message of grace, thus corresponds to the paradoxical basic condition of man. It is the solution of that paradox and the surpassing fulfillment of that condition.

This thesis may also be developed from its other end, for it may not only be shown how grace corresponds to the human condition but also how new light falls upon the world from God's self-communicating love. God's self-revelation and self-communication in history show us first who God is. God can indeed only communicate himself in the history of our salvation because from eternity he is self-communication in love—that is, because from eternity he is triune. Not long ago the teaching on the Trinity appeared to many like beating a dead horse; they were of the opinion that, practically speaking, one could do nothing more with it than, at best, play with academic difficulties. Since then the situation in both Catholic and Protestant theology has changed completely. Trinitarian teaching is being asked for everywhere once again. On closer inspection the trinitarian confession is nothing other than the theological, even if stammering, paraphrase of the words in the First Letter of John: "God is love" (1 Jn 4:8, 16). By this is meant that God is no monomaniacal, solitary God; he is, rather, dialogical within himself and the self-communication of love within himself; he is communion with himself. But if the highest, all-embracing and all-determining being that we call God is love, then all of reality is determined by love and oriented to love; then love is the meaning of all reality.

A thesis such as this has important consequences for our Christian understanding of reality. The trinitarian community/unity appears as a model for the Christian understanding of reality. The teaching on the Trinity signifies a breakthrough from an understanding of reality that was stamped by the primacy of a substance that existed in and for itself to an understanding of reality that is marked by the primacy of person and relation. According to Christian thought, the ultimate reality is conceivable not in terms of a self-subsistent substance but of a person who is fulfilled only in a selfless relationality of giving and

receiving. It could also be said that the meaning of
being, from the Christian point of view, is love.

A "trinitarian ontology" of this sort can of
course not be established compellingly in a purely
inductive way. Mere assertion, blind facticity,
abstract historicity and ultimate meaninglessness
of reality constantly come to the surface and want
to contradict such an explanation. This viewpoint,
nonetheless, is plausible because it can integrate
experiences of reality that at first appear contra-
dictory and because it need not do violence to
anything thereby. Inasmuch as love does not ab-
sorb the other but rather receives him as other,
this explanation can also incorporate and let stand
experiences of reality that fit into no system—
guilt, loneliness, sadness over one's finitude,
failure. It does not stay there, however. It says,
instead, that the ultimate meaning of all reality is
love and that, therefore, everything that happens
in love and out of love becomes permanent. Everything else disappears, but love remains forever
(see 1 Cor 13:8). Therefore the fruits of love will
also have permanence.

From this comes the fundamental model of a
Christian spirituality of selfless service. The Persons of the Trinity are in fact characterized by
their selflessness. Each is in his way pure self-
donation, pure self-emptying. Their existence,
kenotic from all eternity, is the condition for the

possibility of the Son's kenosis in time. It is by the same token the paradigm of Christian humility and of selfless Christian service. It is not power and splendor but rather service and humility that are the "places of being"—places where the ultimate and the enduring even now make their home.

Out of this Christian view of reality there arise consequences having to do not only with personal existence but also with the realm of the political. Monotheism has always been a political program, as evidenced in the old German slogan: "One God, one realm, one king". When one recognizes this, then one understands why the Roman emperors took such a long time to acknowledge the orthodox teaching on the Trinity and why, by contrast, they favored the Arian confession, with its belief in a unified being that was closed off in itself and detached. The Church's teaching on the Trinity presents a completely different picture of unity. This is no rigid, monolithic, uniform and tyrannical unity that shuts out or sucks up and overwhelms all differences of being. Unity of this sort would be poverty. God's unity is a fullness, and indeed an excess, of selfless giving and bestowal, of loving self-outpouring; it is a unity that includes rather than excludes a living, loving being-with and being-for. Thus a particular teaching on the Trinity is the object of a particular political theology that serves in an ideological way as a sanctioning of master-subject relationships, in which an individual or a group attempt to impose their concepts of unity and order and their concerns upon others. The Church's teaching on the Trinity, however, inspires an order in which unity results because all have a part in what is their own, thereby making it common. That is as far removed from collectivism as it is from individualism. For community does not remove one's own being and one's own rights but rather fulfills them in the bestowal of one's own and in the receiving of the other's. Community is of persons, and it preserves the primacy of each individual person. Each finds his fulfillment not in an individualistic having but in giving and, with this, in the sharing of what is one's own.

This trinitarian understanding of unity as community/unity also has consequences for the correct understanding of the unity of the Church. Our traditional understanding of the Church's unity is basically still pretrinitarian. Only when we have understood and brought about unity as unity in diversity shall we have taken utterly seriously the ecclesiological consequences of the trinitarian confession.

K. Hemmerle has set out the consequences for Christian spirituality of a community/unity of this sort. This spirituality is contemplative, for it is attentive to the traces of love that it comes across

in all of reality, but particularly in the cross of
Jesus Christ. The self-giving of God in Jesus Christ
is not only the basis for but also the enduring
measure of this spirituality, to which it looks,
time and again, in order to make it its own. This
spirituality is therefore both active and secular in
its contemplation. It concurs in God's self-giving
for mankind. Thus it is directed toward service in
the world and for the world. This spirituality,
finally, is communitarian and ecclesial in its contemplation and action. It lives out of mutuality. It
is not inclined toward the pleasure and disposition
of the individual; rather it esteems interrelationship in the true sense of that term.

This, then, is a far cry from the words of
Schleiermacher to the effect that the teaching on
the Trinity could be what it may but that it would
have no bearing on the rest of the faith. Instead, it
is the presupposition and the summation of the
whole. It is already at work in creation, when God
lovingly gives participation in his own being. It is
at work to a still higher degree in the redemption
and liberation from the power of evil and in the
order of grace, in which we are taken into the
trinitarian life of God. To sum up: the trinitarian
confession implies that the meaning of being is
love. Faith in the triune God is consequently at
work in loving activity. Faith thus has a power
that opens up and transforms reality. It is reality-

embracing. It is rooted in and lives out of a reality that endures.

It is good for us Christians to let ourselves be questioned by others. But in the end we may ourselves ask: Where else shall we go? Where else do we meet such words of life? The glory of God is the life and salvation of man.

VII

The Community of Believers

One Does Not Believe in *the Church*

Many difficulties with faith are difficulties with the Church. Hardly any other phrase of the Creed meets such opposition and irritation as the confession of one, holy, catholic and apostolic Church. In fact, each of these lofty predicates seems to be given the lie in reality. The Church, as we experience her, is neither unified nor completely holy; looked at empirically, she is not all-embracingly catholic, and she seems in many respects to be far removed from her apostolic origins. Even apart from this the Church can be confronted with a long list of sins, both past and present. Whoever makes claims as high as the Church does will be judged by those claims, even though he can never do complete justice to them; he places himself under the judgment of his own claims. Thus the objections are encountered time and again that the Church does not herself live and practice what she preaches and, indeed, that she has often even betrayed the gospel of God's love. When it is a question of the Church as the community of believers, then tense and self-critical observations are made from the very start.

Even the ancient credal formulas express themselves reservedly with respect to the Church. They say: "I believe in one God, . . . in one Lord, Jesus Christ, . . . in the Holy Spirit." They generally do not say, however: "I believe *in* the Church", but only: "I believe the Church." They thus make it clear that the Church is not the end of the act of faith. The end and the real object of the act of faith is the trinitarian God alone. The Church has her place within and, to a certain degree, under faith in God. The Church is not God; she is a created entity that must never be absolutized and idolized. Such absolutizing is, indeed, a constant temptation for the Church. Inasmuch as the Church is a created entity and consists in sinful human beings, one cannot give her the radical submission that one gives to God in faith. One does not believe *in* the Church, but one believes *within* the Church (de Lubac); one believes *the* Church as the locus of faith and as the community of believers. Now this must be developed and established in detail.

One Believes within *and* with *the Church*

Even if the Church is not the end of the act of faith, she nonetheless has a firm place in the Creed. One cannot simply say Yes to God and Jesus and No to the Church! Faith and the Church essentially belong together.

From the purely human point of view, no one lives all alone. As men, we are dependent on one another in numerous ways. That is true not only with respect to the satisfaction of our elementary bodily needs or the procurement of food and clothing, homes to live in and work for our daily support. Even in our moral and religious convictions we live off what we have received from our parents and teachers, from friends and acquaintances and, in short, from our environment. Our own thoughts require language, and, again, we express our thoughts in language. But we take our language from the community in which we were raised and in which we live. Along with our language we take up the determinative patterns of meaning from around us. As a language-using being man is a social creature.

God is a God of men. Therefore he never speaks in his revelation only to isolated individuals. He speaks, rather, to individuals in their social network. He calls and gathers a people. That began with Adam, who was the representative of the whole human race. When Adam's renunciation of God also brought about enmity between men, starting with Cain's murder of Abel and going up to the Babylonian confusion of tongues, God started anew with a collective movement. According to the Fathers of the Church, this began with righteous Abel and continued with all those who lived righteously and devoutly in accordance with their consciences. It became visible with Abraham, whom God made the father of a great nation and in whom he blessed all nations, and with Moses and the prophets. Jesus himself knew that he was called to gather together the people of Israel. After Israel had renounced this in its majority and in its authoritative representatives, after the death of Jesus, after Easter and Pentecost, a new collective movement began, to which now both Jews and Gentiles belong. They gather in common faith in the one God and in the one Lord and Savior Jesus Christ, in the one Holy Spirit, and they know that they are one another's brothers and sisters, among whom all differences of nationality, race and sex have lost their divisive and discriminating significance.

The Church as the people of God, gathered together in brotherly fashion out of all peoples, races and sexes, is thus God's counteraction against the chaos that has arisen out of sin. This becomes even clearer as God's history with men proceeds. She is the beginning, the sign and the instrument of the peace and reconciliation that God promised and that all people are yearning for. In her a divided and alienated humanity is again reunited in the fundamental convictions and directions of life; in her strangers become friends. Thus the Church herself is an essential fruit of God's saving activity and, to that extent, also a part of faith. God's reconciling word—so must it be said in paraphrase of a famous comment by Martin Luther—cannot exist without God's people, just as God's people cannot exist without God's word, through which it is called together and in whose confession it is united.

Inasmuch as the Church as the community of believers is so closely connected with the word of God, there can be no legitimate private Christianity. Faith, to be sure, is the untransferable personal decision of every individual. But this personal act of faith at the same time means entering into the wider history and the wider community of faith. In the ancient Christian creeds, therefore, it says both "I believe" and "we believe". The individual is never alone in his personal faith. We receive the faith from those who believed before us, and in faith we are supported by the whole community of believers. One always believes in and with the Church.

Since the Church is the all-encompassing subject of faith, *sentire ecclesiam* is part of that faith. This is a feeling with and for the Church, a sense of the Church. It consists not in saying Amen to everything that is in the Church but rather in a feeling for what is right and important in the Church. An ecclesial sense can include open and honest criticism, but it rejects all sophisticated "clever" and arrogant faultfinding. It expresses itself rather in respect for the teaching and practice of the Church as well as in a concern to understand her and in an openness to what the Spirit is saying to the community (see Rev 2:7).

The Church as Sign and Instrument

The connection between the Church and faith in God's word can be established in a still more profound way. The word of God has as its goal that people should find it, hear it, accept it and witness to it. It only comes into the world when it finds believing hearts and believing witnesses. If it were not accepted by a community of believers, put into living practice and further witnessed, then it would be a call without an echo; it would remain without strength and effect and would fade away into nothingness. But since God's word is an effective word that brings about what it says, the acceptance of the word of God in faith also always pertains to God's revelation in the word. The Church as a community of believers belongs constitutively, therefore, within the deed of revelation. Apart from the community of believers nothing would have been revealed in history. In the Church and in her faith the word of God, by way of the Spirit of God, takes form in all weakness and frailty. The Church is herself a form of God's word. She is the pillar and foundation of truth (see 1 Tim 3:15). She participates in the mystery of Christ.

Johann Adam Möhler expressed this thought in the following way:

> In the Church and through her, the redemption announced by Christ by means of the Spirit has become real, since in her his truths are believed and his teachings practiced, and precisely in this way they have come alive. We can accordingly also say of the Church that she is the Christian religion become objective, its living portrayal. Inasmuch as the word spoken by Christ (understood in the broadest terms) entered with his Spirit into a group of human beings and was received by them, it has taken on a shape and flesh and blood. This shape is precisely the Church, which is considered by Catholics to be the essential form of the Christian religion itself. Inasmuch as the Redeemer, through his word and his Spirit, founded a community in which he let his word come to life, he also confided this word to its protection and propagation. He placed his word in it so that it would come forth from it always the same but ever new and with ever fresh strength, so that it would proliferate and

take firm hold. His word is never again separable from the Church, nor his Church from the word.

Möhler also obviously knew that the Church, since she was composed of men who were sinners, reflected the word of God in manifold ways but only brokenly. The Second Vatican Council, therefore, avoids every direct identification of the Church and Jesus Christ, who is *the* Word of God. The Council, rather, refers to the Church as a sacrament —that is, as a sign and instrument. She is the living, full and effective sign of the word of God that has been proclaimed, and at the same time she is its instrument, by which that word may remain clear in the history of the world and of man.

It is not only the offices in the Church that are sign and instrument. All believers and all the baptized are, as individuals and as a whole, intended to be witnesses of faith. Cardinal Newman, in his famous essay *On Consulting the Faithful in Matters of Doctrine*, pointed out that in the strife-ridden fourth century, in which there was conflict over the divinity of Christ, it was frequently not the bishops and episcopal synods that preserved the true faith, but rather the simple faithful. Today in a particular way the time of the Christian laity has arrived. For only through the laity, who live out day-to-day relationships in family, job and leisure, can faith reach the world and prevail from within.

The whole community of believers is the sign and instrument of faith not only through the word, not only through preaching, catechesis and religious instruction, but also through its whole life. A witness is, indeed, defined by the fact that he does not witness merely with his mouth but with his whole existence. He gives of himself and, in extreme cases, even sets his own life on the line. Thus, in the words of the Second Vatican Council, the Church is a sign and instrument through everything that she is and everything that she believes. On her face, the light, who is Jesus Christ, must shine in the world.

The Church under the Word of God

As the history of the Church reveals, the Church can also, in fact, obscure Christ and his word. She can even, at times and in part, become an anti-sign and the whore of Babylon in her external appearance.

Against the background of such terrible conditions in the Church, which are hardly conceivable anymore, it is understandable why Luther and the other Reformers turned to the witness of the Gospel, as it appears in Scripture, and declared that Scripture alone (*sola scriptura*) was the norm for all the Church's discourse and activity. For them the Church under the word of God was a Church that was always in need of reform from the Gospel (*ecclesia semper reformanda*).

The Council of Trent rejected the principle of "Scripture alone" and defended the authoritative character of tradition. In fact, Holy Scripture is not isolated from the living tradition; it is itself, rather, a product of the tradition of the earliest communities. It has its context in the Church. Since it came out of the life of the Church and was written for the life of the Church, it can only be properly understood and interpreted by someone who is himself rooted in the life of the Church—which means, in her tradition. But the correct interpretation is a decisive matter, for Scripture itself is of little use; all Christian churches and movements appeal to it. It is a question of interpreting Scripture correctly. This is only possible for someone who stands and lives in the same ecclesial life context as that out of which Scripture arose. Only someone who himself celebrates the Last Supper, for example, will fully understand the Last Supper accounts of the New Testament, which are themselves witnesses of the earliest liturgy. That is the deeper reason why Catholic teaching sees Scripture and tradition as so closely interconnected. Today a far-reaching consensus among the churches is taking shape in this respect.

A consensus is also taking shape today in Catholic

theology in particular, which is emphasizing that the Church, without prejudice to what may have been said before, stands not over but under the word of God. As early as the Council of Trent the distinction was made between the original and permanently enduring apostolic tradition and human traditions in the Church, which are not only changeable but can also contradict or obscure the original apostolic tradition. Thus not everything that is commonly taken to be traditional in the Church is equally binding and unchangeable. On the contrary, the numerous different traditions must constantly be measured against the tradition of apostolic witness that was handed down once for all. Thus it was that Trent could introduce one of the most important reforms in the history of the Church. The Second Vatican Council made this aspect and the significance that it has for Scripture still clearer when it spoke of the fact that the Church must continue along the path of purification and renewal.

The Church is indeed convinced that God's word and God's truth were given to her in a permanent way. But she knows at the same time that this truth is so exalted and so rich that she cannot exhaust it with any of her doctrinal statements. Such statements are true, to be sure, in what they say, but their power of expression, as in the case of all human words, is limited. Thus, with regard to doctrinal statements, for every likeness there is a still greater unlikeness between what is said and what is intended. Every doctrinal statement transcends itself. The act of faith, as Thomas Aquinas says, aims not at a statement as such but rather by means of the statement at what is intended by it, the actual "object" of faith, which is the mystery of the triune God. Every doctrinal statement can therefore be deepened. It goes without saying that much in the Church that obstructs and obscures the true intention of the Church's doctrinal statements must be purified and renewed.

To believe within and with the Church is not to lay the groundwork for any fixed ideological standpoint or for any ecclesial triumphalism. Rather, to believe within and with the Church means to proceed along the path of continual conversion and of an ever-new attentiveness to the word of God. It is not only the faith of the individual that is a journey; the faith of the Church is also a journey and a process, which often enough leads through questions, crises and convulsions. That is not only true today; in the Church's past as well there were developments and radical changes that brought with them a clarification, for the first time, of the exact content of the Church's faith. To be believing and Catholic does not mean to be undisturbed and certainly not to be proud and self-righteous about all these difficulties but rather to journey with the whole community of believers and to contribute, to the measure of one's talents, to the clarification and deepening of the faith. Precisely as a pilgrim Church that is herself repentant can she be credible in a new way.

An Infallible Church?

Thus far we have developed two points of view in particular. The good news of ultimate salvation has *already* come into the world in the Church, and it remains present there. But the Church is *not yet* the kingdom of God in its perfection; she is, along with her witness to the faith, still en route. This tension has a fundamental significance if we now raise the question of the ultimacy and immutability of the Church's doctrinal statements and of the infallibility of her doctrinal definitions.

The infallibility of the Church in matters of faith and morals creates significant difficulties for many people in our day. They see in this a rigidity and an immobility that are, in their estimation, a great disadvantage, especially today, in the face of the rapidly increasing advances in knowledge and the swift changes in every area of life.

But let us look first at the positive aspects. It is precisely in the tidal wave of verbiage characteristic of our time, in the variability of world views, in the breathtaking developments everywhere and in the restlessness and frenzy of the age that, as men, we need a place where we can stand still and drop anchor. We need "something" that is ultimately reliable, a space where we are at home. In precisely this situation it is beneficial for us when the Church tells us in her solemn pronouncements and also guarantees what she says: If you stand fast in this truth, then you will not go astray, you will remain on course, you are in the truth that endures and that has permanency. To be sure, strictly speaking, only God is infallible; he alone is the foundation for our faith. But God, who has revealed himself in Christ, gives his Church, in the Holy Spirit, a participation in his truth—that is, in his permanency and solidity. He gives the Church in her offices, and particularly in the Petrine office, a mouth, so to speak, by which she can speak in a binding manner. Such an unequivocal and binding quality belongs to the essence of the faith, in which the ultimate breaks into the midst of the temporal. Without firm and unerring statements the faith, in its inmost substance, would disappear.

In the last two hundred years, since the emergence of a greater historical awareness, another aspect has also become clearer: infallible doctrinal definitions have a part not only in the "already" but also in the "not yet" of the reality of salvation. As enduringly

true as they may be in what they say, they nonetheless express this truth in historical and human
words and images whose power of expression is
limited. These statements are, moreover, usually
determined by, directed toward and formulated
with respect to a particular error. Consequently
they often have only one aspect in view; they by
no means intend to say everything. They must
therefore be interpreted within the framework of
the wider total witness of Scripture and tradition.
In this way a broadening and deepening can take
place; in certain circumstances what was intended
can be formulated later in a better and more com-
prehensive way. Thus the development of a doctrine does not conclude with a solemn doctrinal
definition; after the definition the process of interpretation usually begins. This process is entrusted not only to theology but to the whole
community of believers as well. Only in the faith
and life of the whole community does what is
spiritually fruitful in an official dogmatic definition
finally appear.

The significance of the Church's solemn doctrinal definitions should be neither overvalued and
fixated upon nor undervalued. These definitions
are relatively infrequent and extraordinary occur-
rences in the Church's life, but they are rooted in
her day-to-day life, faith and preaching. Many
central truths of faith, especially the Apostles'

Creed, were never formally defined but nonetheless stand very firmly upon the common faith of the Church. That makes it clear once more that the real subject of faith is not an individual, not even an individual in an official capacity, but rather the whole community of believers in the unity and multiplicity of their charisms, services and offices. The truth of the gospel is infallibly entrusted, with the assistance of the Holy Spirit, to the totality of believers and to their consensus.

The Community of Faith Concretely Understood

The statement that has just been made brings us to a final question: Is today's Church ever actually still experienced as a community? Is she really a place in which the individual Christian is at home, or is she felt to be a distant institution? The question probably cannot be answered with one general response. People's experiences are too different. Nonetheless, the ideal that the New Testament shows us, particularly in the primitive Jerusalem community, is unambiguous.

When we look in the New Testament under the heading of "Church", we discover not one but three different meanings. In the first place there is the Church in the sense in which we usually understand the term today—as universal, as a world

Church. But in numerous places in the New Testament Church also means the Church in a particular place—the local church. It was widely identified at the time with a community and did not mean merely a section or a jurisdiction of the universal Church but rather the actualization and representation of the Church in a concrete place. The unity of the universal Church in antiquity was a community/network of such relatively independent local churches. Today the local church in its fullest sense is only understood to be the diocese under the leadership of the bishop. But the title of church can be given analogously to the local community or the parish; at least this is the case in more recent theology of the community. In the community, indeed, the experience of place cedes to that of church. It is here that the concrete rooting and being at home must occur. But there is still a third meaning that is important in the New Testament —the Church as house church, the community that is gathered in the house of a Christian or of a Christian family (see Rom 16:5, 23; 1 Cor 16:19; Philemon 2; Col 4:15). In a certain sense it can even be said that the earliest Church established herself in "house" fashion.

The ideal image of such brotherly community is the primitive Jerusalem community: "All those who believed lived together and had everything in common. They sold their goods and possessions and from this gave to everyone as each had need. They went to the Temple every day, broke bread in their houses and ate together in joy and simplicity of heart" (Acts 2:44–46).

This system of house churches continued in principle in the early Church until the Constantinian era. Only after the time of persecution, when the Church was legalized as a religious community and later even recognized as the state religion, was it possible and even necessary, for prudent and practical reasons, to erect large church buildings. Today in many Third World churches, not only in Latin America but also in Africa, there is once more an option in favor of small communities, which are often referred to as base communities. Pope Paul VI and the Roman bishops' synod of 1985 have remarked that these communities are a great hope for the universal Church. In them a Church that is otherwise felt to be anonymous can once again be experienced and lived out concretely as a community of faith—in the common reading and interpretation of Holy Scripture, in common praying and singing, in Christian instruction, in common concern in the face of concrete emergencies. This is possible in all sorts of ways, in different groups, circles, movements, religious orders and church societies and sodalities.

Without insertion into a particular community

of believers, it is becoming increasingly difficult to be a Christian and to maintain one's Christian faith in today's world. The handing on of the faith to the next generation is also absolutely dependent on such faith communities. Thus they deserve a high pastoral priority.

Certainly the danger of sectarianism and partisan wrangling should not be underestimated. This danger, it is clear from the First Letter to the Corinthians, already existed in New Testament times. The determinative consideration, therefore, is that the individual communities not live next to one another in isolated fashion or, indeed, be in adversary positions with respect to one another. A legitimate and authentic community of Jesus Christ can only be such if it is in communion with all the other communities in which Jesus Christ is likewise present (see Mt 18:20). But the positive possibilities —as well as the dangers—in the option in favor of small communities should also be seen. These should be used as an occasion to achieve a renewal and an enlivening of the biblical and early Christian image of the Church—the Church as a concretely experienced community of faith, more than a place, in worldwide communication within the one universal Church.

A Church thus understood and lived as community could, once again, be experienced more clearly as a sign and instrument of salvation for the world. Upon her face the light of Christ would shine brighter and clearer as the light of the world and of man. Thus Christian faith could take on a new shape in our day.